Praise for *Peace & Energy* ...

"This book is incredibly helpful for those who have experienced abuse in their lives, particularly as children. It is highly accessible—no medical or psychological jargon—and the analogies help explain the concepts being introduced. Highly recommended!"

— Jamie McMillin, Author, *Legendary Learning*

"Mariane Weigley's third book continues with new insights into understanding dissociation and negative energy, portrayed with a depth that is riveting. By deeply examining her stories of loss, she gained an awareness of energy that she has applied to overcome gripping circumstances. She conveys what's possible if we understand how the human energy system works—and how to clean it up when it's blocked, torn, and fragmented. This whole series offers tremendous hope for traumatized people to mend, reintegrate, and find peace."

— Janice DeCovnick, PhD, Clinical Psychologist
Member, American Psychological Association

"Energy in the Universe is constantly there for healing. Be open to it."

— Jo Ann Cooper, PhD, Psychologist
Member, American Psychological Association
Diplomate, American Academy of Pain Management
Fellow, American College of Forensic Examiners

"I really liked this book. Not only were the stories a connecting moment to parallel my life, but it was filled with application tools. Very useful!"

— Dana Christiansen, Wife, Mom, Stylist

"The books in this *Abuse & Energy*™ *Series* have given me hope to continue forward in my own life."

— Karen Lee Schmidt, Career-minded Independent Woman

"I liked how you relate the fact that if we can focus on healing ourselves individually, we can then heal as a country. It's an important point and one that interested me the most."

— Elizabeth Yost, Energy Healer, Writer

"This third book brought it all together for me, was positive and helpful . . . you brought forth the joy of healing along with how the reader can heal. 'Survival Mode' hit home for me. It gives a name to when your soul, your energy, is injured and needs to recuperate . . . seeing the 13 characteristics written out with steps to shift out of Survival Mode was beyond beneficial."

— Nancy D. Campbell, Healthcare/IT Professional

One woman's path for healing
after abuse, trauma, and dissociation

PEACE & ENERGY

Becoming the Person
You Always Could Have Been

MARIANE E. WEIGLEY, JD

Book 3, Abuse & Energy™ Series

WEIGLEY PUBLICATIONS, INC.
BROOKFIELD, WISCONSIN

PEACE & ENERGY
Becoming the Person You Always Could Have Been

© 2022 Mariane Weigley, JD

All rights reserved. Except for the quotation of brief passages for review, no portion of this book may be reproduced, stored in a retrieval system, or transmitted in any form or by any means, electronic, mechanical, photocopy, recording, scanning, or other without the prior written permission of the publisher.

Weigley Publications, Inc.
PO Box 765
Brookfield, Wisconsin 53008-0765

www.WeigleyPublications.com
www.MarianeWeigley.com

Important Caution to the Reader: This book does not provide psychological, medical, legal, financial, or other professional advice of any kind. Please consult an appropriate professional for any such advice.

ABUSE & ENERGY (U.S. Reg. No. 5747416) is a trademark of Mariane E. Weigley and is used under license. WEIGLEY PUBLICATIONS and logo are trademarks of Weigley Publications, Inc.

Editor: Barbara McNichol Editorial
Book design: Shannon Bodie, BookwiseDesign.com
Author photo: Diane Yokes of Yokes Photography

ISBNs: 978-0-9884990-4-1 print, 978-0-9884990-5-8 ebook

Printed in the United States of America

Publisher's Cataloging-In-Publication Data
(Prepared by The Donohue Group, Inc.)

Names: Weigley, Mariane E., author.
Title: Peace & energy : becoming the person you always could have been / Mariane Weigley, JD.
Other Titles: Peace and energy
Description: Brookfield, WI : Weigley Publications, Inc., [2022] | Series: Abuse & energy series ; [book 3] | Includes bibliographical references.
Identifiers: ISBN 9780988499041 (print) | ISBN 9780988499058 (ebook)
Subjects: LCSH: Weigley, Mariane E.--Psychology. | Energy psychology. | Self-actualization (Psychology) | Psychological abuse. | Survival--Psychological aspects. | Vital force.
Classification: LCC RC489.E53 W453 2022 (print) | LCC RC489.E53 (ebook) | DDC 616.89--dc23

Dedication

To all of us.

Souls themselves do not have a gender, nor do they have a specific color. Souls can express themselves in a multitude of ways: no color, no race, no gender, no specific religion or faith, and no specific sexual preference can be used to describe a soul. A soul is a soul. It is energy—a being of light—that expresses itself according to the circumstances it finds itself in while in physical form.

Therefore, underneath it all, we are all the same.
We are eternal.
We are Souls. We are Energy.

There is something in every one of you that waits and listens for the sound of the genuine in yourself. It is the only true guide you will ever have. And if you cannot hear it, you will all of your life spend your days on the ends of strings that someone else pulls.

—HOWARD THURMAN, Author, Philosopher,
Theologian, Educator, Civil Rights Leader

Contents

A Note from the Author xiii

Introduction 1

1	Could It Be That John Was Dying, Too?	7
2	John's Passing	19
3	My Family House—The Log Cabin	29
4	A Revealing Diary Hidden From View	41
5	The Presence Of Negative Energy	53
6	When Negative Energy Leaves	61
7	Call It By Its Name—Survival Mode	67
8	Trust Your Natural Instincts	85
9	Listen to Your Intuition	89
10	The Value of Setting Intentions	95
11	Learn to "See" and "Hear" Properly	105
12	Supporting Your Energy System	117
13	The Need for Energy Safety	125
14	Trust the Epiphanies That Come to You	131
15	Notice Timing Is Critical	137
16	Circuitry, Chakras, and Connections	145
17	EnergySpeak—The Language of Life	157
18	What Feeds Your Soul	161
19	What You *Don't* Know Can Be the Problem	173

20	Learn to Journal and Meditate	177
21	What to Say to Others and What They Might Say to You	181
22	Tell Your Story With Universal Rules of Energy in Mind	185
23	Peace Begins on the Inside and Nowhere Else	191
24	Restore the Human Energy System	197
25	Rise	209

Glossary 215

Acknowledgments 219

Appendix—Stories In Books 1 & 2 221

Recommended Resources 225

About The Author 237

Stories

A number of pivotal stories in *Peace & Energy* are meant to become teaching references for you. Look for these stories as you read:

Narrative Story from Books 1 and 2	2
The Speedboat	8
The Urgent Email	10
The Missing Key	16
The Missing Key Found	17
John and the Guardian	23
His Funeral	26
Mom's Jewelry Under the Living Room Floorboards	32
Breaking into the Family Safe	34
Dad's Office	35
John's Bedroom	36
Mom's Hidden Diary Found	42
Suicide Thoughts at Age Fifteen (Revisited)	50
The First Wife's Energy	54
John's Trauma	55
Mom's Energy	56
Dark Energy at the Apartments	57
Mom's Cookbook Mysteriously Found	57

Black Flies Surrounding Mom's Buick	58
The Release of Toxins and Tears	63
The High School Bus (Finding the Log Cabin Girl)	75
Closing the Coffin Lid (Finding the Office Girl)	77
The Lumberyard Kids	79
The Linn Pier Close Call	82
Tell Your Analytical Mind to Get in the Back Seat So the Rest of You Can Drive	91
"What Needs to be Said"	96
"I Don't Have a Life"	99
Which Coffee Cup in the Morning	106
A Conversation with "Dad"—a Grief Unfolding	108
My Foundational Personal Energy Needs	120
Wait for the Signal	138
The 4-Cup Measuring Cup	142
Sequel to Finding the Office Girl—January 2020	146
Sequel to the Lumberyard Kids—January 2021	147
I Just Got Here—An Eight-year-old Lumberyard Kid—February 2021	150
The Letter "L"	154
Bringing Home the Bacon	163
Making My Beef Stew	166
My Christmas Eve Engagement	174
The Blue Sleeping Bag	178
The Chevy, Workhorse, and Sting	186
Things I Had to Learn the Hard Way—When the Bottom Falls Out	201
A Wall of Spices 2001 (Revisited in 2020)	204
A Wall of Spices (Original)	207
Coming Around the Bend—An Obituary	210

A Note from the Author

IF YOU ARE LIKE MANY READERS, YOU MIGHT CONSIDER jumping right to Chapter One and begin reading. I want to ask you (especially if you're a first-time reader of this series) to take a few minutes and read my **Introduction** first. It uniquely sets the stage for what follows and gets you acclimated (or reacclimated) to the story line. It also underscores how visual imagery can show up in many ways and carry significant healing with it.

My stories and thoughts reveal how healing worked for me. I realize that each of us is in a different emotional place, and we've had different experiences. However, despite our varied circumstances, showing you how I healed from abuse, trauma, and dissociation is meant to help facilitate your own path to health.

What my path looks like is shown graphically here. This visual came to me during my early journaling and became a kind of North Star. It gradually filled in and showed me where I was, what I needed to know (in general), and where my life could go. Writing Books 1 and 2—*Abuse & Energy* and *Deep Energy*—was a significant part of my healing journey. Realizing I had unprocessed grieving to finish and that I had held my own energy inside for years was part of my journey, too. This visual helped me understand that something was wrong. But it also showed me that it could be made right.

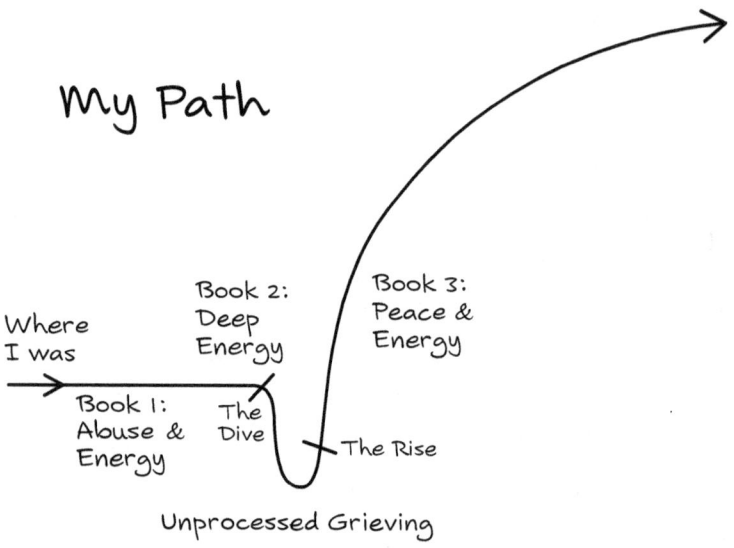

My Energetic Reaction to Abuse & My Path Upward

On a different point, you might use the word Emotion as a more familiar substitute for Energy when building your knowledge and experience of Energy through this *Abuse & Energy Series*. Yet, Energy is infinitely broader than Emotion. That's why I strongly encourage you to expand your understanding of Emotion/Energy by reading all three books in this series. If you go to **www.WeigleyPublications.com**, you will find helpful links to Amazon, Barnes & Noble, and IndieBound (local independent bookstores).

Look for these titles:

- *Abuse & Energy: Bringing You Home Through the Transformational Power of Energy*
- *Deep Energy: Diving into the Depths of Your Personal Understanding*
- *Peace & Energy: Becoming the Person You Always Could Have Been*

Mariane Weigley, JD

Introduction

SOME TIME AGO, I SENSED THAT HOW I REBOUNDED from the damage left by my childhood experience of abuse is filled with insights that can be applied universally. It evolved into an approach that informs, validates, and supports individuals going through trauma.

Describing my own intense self-examination began with Books 1 and 2 of the *Abuse & Energy Series* and is explored further in Book 3, *Peace & Energy*. As a lawyer, I am trained to look for the bigger picture derived by paying close attention to details. In this series, the details reflect my life. The more I looked, the more I realized the details of my overall story could be used in helping a nation to heal—for a *nation* under stress is made up of *individuals* under stress.

Taken as a whole, the stories you'll read have been carefully crafted using Energy/Emotion as a guiding light—the kind of energy that overcomes separation due to abuse and ultimately supports a way of living that's peaceful inside. Hence, Peace is part of the title. As the lyric from a popular hymn goes, "Let there be peace on earth, and let it begin with me."

Through these chapters and the stories within them, you have the potential of embracing your own guiding light or

Flashlight—one you can turn on to inform, validate, and support YOU as you internalize messages about how energy works in your life. You'll find the concept of the Flashlight introduced in Chapter Six. Preceding it are chapters that continue the narrative laid out in Books 1 and 2. The story that follows includes key milestones from these two books to help you "catch up" before you dive into Chapter One of *Peace & Energy*.

Scattered throughout the book, you'll also find contemplation questions to ask yourself. They're meant to help you achieve what I call actionable clarity—personal insights uniquely yours that will lead you to action.

> *Throughout the book, you'll find questions to help you achieve personal insights that will lead to action.*

Narrative Story from Books 1 and 2

In the late summer of 1983, I was living in Fond du Lac, Wisconsin, with my husband and our two children. He'd accepted a new job two-and-a-half hours away in Rockford, Illinois, just over the Wisconsin-Illinois border. We couldn't move right away; there was a recession, and we had a house to sell in Fond du Lac. So, he started his job and commuted home on weekends.

The following spring, we sold our house, but before that, we searched for housing near his new company's location. We found nothing affordable in the school district we wanted, so my mother presented us with an opportunity. She and my brother John lived a 45-minute drive from where my husband worked. She offered to let us rent a house my deceased father had built years before. Yes, that commute was doable. Because we were paying for a dishwasher and other fixups, she gave us the first year rent-free. After that, we'd have to pay market rent, my mother said. The plan? I would work in the family real estate business that my father had started and was now run by my mother and brother.

My husband liked the whole idea. As for me, living in my hometown of Lake Geneva would be a challenge. I had sworn I'd never go back. Indeed, I could feel myself screaming inside at the idea of returning. Finally, I agreed to do it. Why? Because I could *hear* a soft little voice inside quietly saying, "It's the right thing to do."

My Family Dynamics

My family stayed in Lake Geneva four years. However, during that time, nothing in our family dynamics had changed involving me, my mother, and my brother. Did I start working in the business? After two days of Mom showing me the ropes, no. She stopped, and I did, too. My best guess for why she did that? John got wind of what we were doing.

In 1985, my husband and I considered building a home and looked for land near Rockford, Illinois. Ultimately, it came down to whether we wanted to move to Illinois or stay in Wisconsin. Neither of us could decide. But then I said, "All I know is if we were to flip a coin and it came up 'Illinois,' then I would want to go for two out of three flips, but I couldn't tell you why." He felt the same way. It was a fortuitous decision steered by subtle feelings.

In 1986, he changed jobs, this time moving to a company near Milwaukee, so he commuted north from our rented home in Lake Geneva.

Right Thing to Do?

Was moving back to my hometown the right thing to do? Was the soft little voice I heard correct? Yes.

We left Lake Geneva two years later and moved to Waukesha near Milwaukee. I listened carefully. And I honored an epiphany I'd had in late 1986—that I needed to go to law school *in order to become the person I always could have been.*

The week I turned 40, I started classes at Marquette University Law School, graduating four years later. Three years after that, following 25 years of marriage, I filed for divorce.

In 1997, I began to journal and meditate as I worked with a spiritual counselor. I also began regular counseling through the Employee Assistance Program at my work. In late 2000, I began adding color back into my life, starting with painting my toes for the first time in years. And in January 2001, two movies caught my attention: *Castaway* with Tom Hanks and *Chocolat*, the French version, with Juliette Binoche. After I'd seen both movies, things began to happen.

On February 3rd that year, I lined up three Hershey kisses— the traditional silver-wrapped ones—on the coffee table in my apartment. It was a cold, Wisconsin Saturday night. I lit a candle and set my cell phone to dial 911—if needed. Then I ate one of the kisses.

You see, I'd been allergic to chocolate since I was six years old. Dad always had Hershey chocolate bars on the file cabinet in his office, but I couldn't eat any of them after this allergy started. No chocolate birthday cakes. No chocolate for 47 years! But after watching those two movies, I had this epiphany: "I can eat chocolate again, and I'll be fine." I TRUSTED this was right.

That night, I ate two of the pieces. No reaction. I ate the third one the next morning. Then I ate a chocolate treat every day for the next 10 days. My body reacted by releasing lots of toxins.

Facing My Childhood Emotional Abuse

This incident signaled the tip of an iceberg that I gradually understood over the next 19 years. I did not know how devastating this "iceberg" could be, both personally and financially. I do now. It represented the emotional abuse I'd experienced as a child. It came in the form of withholding, enabling, neglect, and isolation, which is detailed in Book 1, *Abuse & Energy*. I had reacted to this abuse with dissociation, allergy, and fragmentation. It all added up to realizing I was *only 15 to 20 percent of who I could have been*. This dissociation, allergy, and fragmentation didn't *begin* to change until I went to law school in 1988 when that number immediately rose to about 40 percent.

What does it mean to get to 100 percent of who you could be?

You feel different.

You act differently.

You experience empathy because the ability to feel fully has returned.

Before, you weren't all there; now, you are.

You are being YOU—100 percent.

That makes a difference for living a better life.

My Journey After "Chocolate"

Between my "chocolate" release in 2001 and now, significant milestones marked my journey, including the deaths of my mother in 2005 and brother in 2013. My reaction to my mother's death was detailed in Book 1. Book 2 marks my return to Wisconsin in 2017 after releasing much of the unprocessed grief that had held me back since my father's death in 1965. What follows in Book 3 details what led to even more energetic recovery and the return of even more fragments on the way to becoming the person I was always meant to be.

It begins with my brother's last few weeks of life.

1

Could It Be That John Was Dying, Too?

*Unprocessed grieving and all its unresolved
issues can linger for years.*

IN LATE JANUARY AND ALL OF FEBRUARY 2013—FOUR months before my brother John died—I kept feeling a sense of urgency, a kind of "hurry up" message. Where did it come from?

By then, I had moved to San Francisco to be near my daughter. As I hastily set up my apartment, I believed it was my brother I was sensing. Apparently, he was getting sick, yet I knew nothing about it from him. Then I had a vision. About him. And me.

The Speedboat Story

The morning of Thursday, March 21, 2013, a vision woke me up about 7:30 a.m. In the vision, I was back in Wisconsin at Dad's office in a lakeshore subdivision he had established in the 1950s. Dad used one of the homes there as a field office where we kept a boat alongside a private pier we maintained.

I felt I was walking toward the lake and our pier across the front lawn of the field office house. Someone (I sensed it was John, my only sibling) walked behind me. The scene felt familiar. Years ago, we'd often take out our boat to go waterskiing. In the vision, I sensed the distinctive sound we made on the boards of that pier with each step.

We both walked with a sense of purpose. I immediately went to the farthest point on the pier. There, I could reach the electrical up/down button for the hoist that controlled the back end of our Century Coronado inboard speedboat. John went to the control button for the bow of the boat. It was important to press both buttons at the same time so the boat could be lowered evenly to the water below. We pressed them in unison.

Once the boat settled onto the water, John unhitched both of the hoists from the boat, started the engine, and backed it out to allow me to get in. He extended his hand to help me step into the back of the boat. I was wearing long robes, peach colored. My "spiritual" robes.

No words were spoken, but I knew he was going to drive as usual. From the first moment I saw him, John appeared to be

20 years old—just like he did during his St. Olaf College days, young and healthy. I was about 16 years old—the age when our dad died.

Geneva Lake is long, and from where we began to move, the boat was near the city of Lake Geneva itself. It takes a bit of time to get to the Fontana end of the lake. But this Century speedboat could go fast, and John had the engine wide open. The boat had a half roof, so I could hang onto it while standing in the back. It skimmed the water at a level angle. I could see straight ahead, which made me feel wonderful.

As the boat approached Fontana, it became airborne, up and up like Santa's sleigh would fly. Then it banked sharply to the left—a turn that threw me right out of the boat. In effect, it was releasing me. I felt no malice. Just a gentle "Mariane, you are free" kind of feeling. Then I watched as the boat completed the turn, landing back down on the water's surface, still with its engine wide open. It sped back to the pier at the other end of the lake where we'd come from.

I wanted to see where John would go next, so I "sped" back to the pier, too. I watched as he brought the boat back into the pier's dock area. He secured it, hooking each one of the hoists and then pushing the UP buttons in a staggered way to raise it into a level position.

I watched as John stood on the pier alone. And I watched as he walked off toward land. After only a few steps, I saw him change into the 68-year-old man of present day.

And I woke up.

I wrote down what I had seen but didn't attribute any meaning to it until the following day. The next morning while waking up, I heard, *"Johnny wants to do something to help you do what it is you can do."* It was Mom. She always called him Johnny. Then an urgent email came in the middle of the afternoon on Friday, March 22nd.

The Urgent Email Story

The email said, "Johnny is being taken to the hospital." It came from the wife of one of John's neighbors with instructions for me to call her husband, Lynn Fischer.

"Oh, my God!" I cried out. Shaking, I immediately called Lynn to fill me in.

It was bad, really bad, for John. No one knew exactly what it was, but it looked like he had cancer. Apparently, John had shown signs of illness the summer before but was now in full-blown trouble. Even though my brother, like Mom, wasn't much for doctors, he had gone for tests in the fall, I found out later. But he refused to learn the results. He did nothing. It seemed he just wanted to pass at home where he had lived all those decades with Mom.

When Lynn became aware John was in trouble, he came into the log cabin through the unlocked living room door. He found John in one of the upstairs bedrooms (my old bedroom—the one with the small window in the door) in an unhealthy, unclean state. John wasn't able to walk and couldn't get to the bathroom, Lynn told me. Besides, the house's plumbing hadn't worked well for years.

That Friday, March 22nd, Lynn made the first 911 call for John to be taken to Lakeland Hospital, a 30-minute drive. After considerable discussion with the emergency responders, John agreed to go.

This email was the first I knew of John's health issue. Although Lynn had been keeping a distant eye on my brother, he had missed this turn of events. He also knew how difficult John could be. Even when Lynn was helping, many times John would give him a dirty look as if to say, "What are you doing here?" My brother's difficult demeanor hadn't changed—and wouldn't.

With this information, my family instincts kicked in— that I should come running. But the moment I felt that, I also heard, "Wait. *Walk, don't run back to Wisconsin. He doesn't want your help.*"

I suspect these words came from Mom. I just knew her message felt correct. So, instead of calling United Airlines right away, I digested everything the neighbor had told me. Fortunately, Lynn was at the hospital with John.

As the weekend progressed, I prepared to fly back to Wisconsin for an extended stay—God only knew how long. I sensed flying out on Monday would be the right pace to match the *"walk, don't run"* message.

Saturday evening, I wondered about flights. *Could I even get a seat on Monday? The airlines might be sold out!* So, I checked on pricing for a one-way ticket from San Francisco to Chicago. Lots of flights were available at $506. All of them—every flight—cost

$506! Not cheap, but I knew I had to fly. What stood out were the numbers 506. That was Dad's birthday, May 6th—5-0-6. Holy smokes! *Every single ticket cost $506.* It meant I was being *told* to come home, that I was needed.

Still, something didn't feel quite right about a Monday flight, so I waited. Finally, on Monday night, I felt the nudge to buy a ticket for Tuesday. Yes, there were still seats. And yes, they still cost $506.

I was going home. Because it was time—for both of us.

After being admitted to the hospital, John stayed for several days, refused all treatment, and then checked himself out over the doctor's objections. That was on March 28th. His departure set in motion a frantic search by the police, county officials, our neighbor, and me.

Back at the log cabin—it was unknown how he got there—John was found by police the next day lying on the living room floor, a black five-gallon bucket two feet away where he'd been defecating and urinating. The police report stated John was unable to walk or get around on his own, that he had not been eating or drinking enough fluids, and that neither the water well nor septic system was working. The report also noted John's weight was down to about 130 pounds, even though his height was six-foot-two.

Again, John was in big trouble. But as much as he wanted to, he couldn't be allowed to die at home. So 911 was called and the paramedics carried him out on a bed sheet, never to return to the log cabin.

Need for a Guardian and Medical Care

On April 1st, Walworth County asked for a hearing to place John in a mental hospital, but the hearing never took place. That move was deemed too harsh. Then on April 4th, the county filed an application for John to have a guardian. It said:

> Mr. Syver is unable to make ongoing healthcare and financial decisions in his own best interest as a result of paranoid thinking and obsessional thoughts about his finances. He is unable to care for himself and meet his own needs in his own home as he is non-ambulatory, is very weak, has no working bathroom, the home is unsanitary, he doesn't have home healthcare services, and has refused to finance services or repairs despite being independently wealthy. His medical prognosis is grave and he requires skilled nursing care.

On the same day, a petition was filed to move him to a local care center in Williams Bay. There, he was told if he tried to leave, the police would be called. That made me feel safer.

Even though I had been in Wisconsin since March 26th, it wasn't until April 10th that I actually saw John. Frankly, I just couldn't go near him. Too much was at stake—namely, my sanity. That's why I had lived outside of Wisconsin for the seven years it took for Mom's estate to resolve. During that process, I was warned by her guardian, John Griebel, that my brother was a problem. The guardian was concerned about my safety—and his own.

On Monday, April 8th, I met with the care center staff. The man who would eventually become John's court-appointed guardian—yes, the same John Griebel who had been Mom's guardian—asked me to join in the meeting. It meant a lot for me to be included, given the history of our family. Afterward, I asked the staff if I could see John. I'd hesitated to do so, given how divisive our estate issues had been. I had told him to never call me directly, only through our attorneys. But my only brother was dying, and I didn't want his life to end without seeing him.

My only brother was dying, and I didn't want his life to end without seeing him.

So a female staff member went to John's room to ask his permission for me to visit. I noticed she had a large silver Hershey Kiss container on her desk, reminding me of how my allergy to chocolate finally broke in 2001. To me, it meant I'd be safe visiting John. *Yup, I am in the right place for whatever is going to happen,* I thought.

John's Initial "No" to My Visit

John Griebel and I waited for the staff person to return. We waited and waited. Finally, she came back with his answer: "No." I quickly grabbed my purse and briefcase and left without a word. My brother's answer was not a surprise.

Two days later, I returned for another meeting, this time with John's attending physician who brought us up to speed on his health situation. John Griebel was present, too. Again, I asked if I could see John. Again, it was up to him if he wanted to see me. Interestingly, when a male doctor asked him for permission, John's answer came back within 10 minutes. "Yes," he said, "because she came all that way."

John Griebel looked at me. "Should I come, too?"

"No," I replied. "But do stand outside the door. If I'm not out in fifteen minutes, knock." I felt scared, but something was driving me to push for this visit—alone.

Our Meeting—Gladness and Wariness

The door of John's room was partially ajar, so I knocked and announced myself. He was lying on the bed. He looked ragged, unkempt but clean. I sensed his behavior was difficult for the staff. John hated the dark and the painfully long nights, but he adamantly refused to have nightlights when the staff offered them. He didn't eat much and only drank cranberry juice with ice. He rarely accepted medication. After all, he didn't want to be there. He didn't want to be sick. Plus he didn't want to know any details about his condition.

This was no great homecoming, but John was noticeably glad to see me, and I was glad to see him, too. With the need to download his thoughts, he gave me a recap of all his medical history since the previous November. He referred to me as his only sister and said we always trusted each other. Then he talked about Lynn Fischer, calling him Eagle Eye Fischer. After 15 minutes, I heard John Griebel's knock on the door. "Go ahead and leave," I told him. "I'll be okay."

Still, I sensed a sharp tension in the room. My guard was up; it *had* to be, knowing my brother was notorious at being manipulative and could be dishonest. He chose his words carefully. I knew I needed to be wary. I would not allow any bullying as happened when Mom was dying. And with John confined to this care center, I could enforce that resolve. *His confinement gave me the power to leave whenever I felt the need.*

The Missing Key Story

Sometime in college, I had lost my gold-colored key to our family house, the log cabin. On my first visit with John at the care center, he said he'd misplaced his key to the log cabin and hadn't been able to lock the living room door for some time. So he wanted me, with Lynn's help, to find that key. "I put it in a baggie, but I can't recall where I hid it," he said.

We were to look under the urns outside the living room door. If it wasn't there, we were to go down to the basement and look "on the board." At that moment, I felt a warmth that took me aback. I hadn't heard the phrase "on the board" since we were kids. Yet it wasn't the phrase that gave me a warm feeling; it's that he said it without explaining *what* the board was (a small plywood board that hung by the fuse box with keys hanging on it) or *where* it was (behind the door at the bottom of the stairwell). I didn't need an explanation. And he knew it.

Based on that history alone, it meant we were brother and sister once again—even for a little while.

Have you ever had a moment in which you felt a similar brief connection again with someone important in your life? What did you learn from that experience?

The Missing Key Found Story

After leaving John's room, I called Lynn who agreed to meet me at the log cabin. This would be the first time I had been there since Mom died in 2005. The exceptions were one visit in 2006 and three visits the year before (all three with Burger King burgers in hand for John).

The house was a wreck, even worse than in 2006. Dark inside. Stink in the bathroom. Food—an open can of beans with a spoon in it—on the kitchen table. Still, the furniture was in the same place as always, and the log cabin's distinctive smell was evident.

After first checking the urns for John's lost key, we headed for the basement. It was full of paper goods and canned foods as well as open takeout food containers with half-eaten contents and black garbage bags of trash. Strangely, John had previously asked Lynn to check for the key, but he didn't tell me that. Apparently, I was the cavalry for another attempt. In the past, I'd often find things that others didn't—and John knew that.

As we found various keys in the basement, Lynn ran them up to the living room door to see if they worked. Nope. *Where else would John have stashed a key?* Ah, behind the door between the kitchen and the office! For years, keys for real estate properties

Dad owned in the 1950s and 1960s hung there. So I went through the kitchen and turned right into the office. Lord, another mess. Papers everywhere. I looked on the backside of the door. Lots and lots of keys—mostly keys to properties sold in the 1970s and 1980s. Even hanging there were three sets of keys to Lynn's house when it was still a rental.

Some keys looked promising, so Lynn tried them in the door lock. No luck. Plastic baggie or not, John's key wasn't here.

So where else? I remembered a catch-all silver-colored tray on top of the refrigerator. I walked into the kitchen (looking as grim as the rest of the house) and approached the old refrigerator. Although I'm only five-foot-five, I could easily view whatever was on top.

First, I saw a tray—not the original tray I'd remembered but still full of stuff. Promising! Then my eyes moved toward something closer to me than the tray. OH MY GOD. A single key, gold, all by itself on the top of the refrigerator door. It was centered in front of the rubber gasket. I *knew* that key. Mine, from college days. *Where had it been all this time? And who had placed it there?* I called for Lynn to test the lock with this key. Of course, it worked.

By this time, it was dark, and we had to leave. But at least now I had a key to show John.

We never did find John's missing key. But we did find mine.

2

John's Passing

He died with a measure of dignity.
That's all I could do for him.

WALKING INTO JOHN'S ROOM THE NEXT MORNING, I didn't know what to expect. He marveled at the key I found, remarking that it wasn't his, but it looked new. No one had used it much. He instructed me to make several copies and bring them back to him. But he didn't say who would get one, and he didn't indicate if I should have a copy, let alone keep the original.

When I returned, I held the copies in my hand along with the key I'd found. He reached for them, but I pulled them back. "Who are you going to give these to?" He didn't reply. "Then I'll keep these—one for Lynn, one extra, and the original for me." He gave me some grief, but I stood firm. I knew something was going on behind the scenes that didn't feel right. *Who was trying to involve themselves in this family matter when they weren't family at all?* It felt dark and vibrationally low.

Leaving John's room with all the keys and knowing he had none felt right for me and my children. My instinctual desire to feel safe was working overtime.

Leaving John's room with all the keys and knowing he had none felt right for me and my children. My instinctual desire to feel safe was working overtime.

In one of our first meetings, I had asked John for his cell phone. Its use was clearly tied to people he was talking to whose identity he declined to reveal. I learned from the nurses he was active on it with lots of conversations. All his secretive talks were warning flags that I knew, at a deep level, I had to act on. And I did. So, after giving me grief, he finally handed it over.

Proceeds from Dad's Estate

The first time we visited in the care center, John mentioned I should have received my 25 percent from Dad's estate. In the next meeting, he repeated that and, with sadness in his voice, added that he should have had his, too. Years before, after Dad died, he had signed over his 25 percent to Mom while I had not. He wasn't aware of that, though, until Mom's estate was settled in 2012. A huge blow to him.

Mentions of Dad's estate were the only times the subject of inheritance came up between us, but they conveyed that something had been wrong with Mom all along. I almost cried when John said I should have received my inheritance from Dad—something I never thought he'd say. Then to hear him state it again—submitting he should have had his, too—broke me. I had to choke back my astonishment—and my relief. After all these years, John finally realized, clearly and with knowledge, that Mom had cheated him, too.

How could he have believed what Mom told him about both of our inheritances when it was a lie all along?

It never had to be this way.

Our Visits—Tense and Calculated

Even though we had moments of solidarity, each visit had been tense and calculated. After the first few, we even held hands. But inside, my intuition told me how long to stay, when to leave, and when to come back (usually in two days' time) and stay for only two hours each time. That message came consistently. I honored it. Normally, John did not ask me to stay longer; he just wanted to know when I would return and say precisely when. He'd watch the clock, so I knew I'd better not be one minute late. He treated the care center staff the same way. Again, I honored my word about being on time.

During one of our visits, the issue of having a guardian came up. That person wouldn't be appointed until the third week of May, after a court-scheduled hearing. Before the hearing, John had asked several people to be his guardian. All had declined.

Three weeks earlier, I had returned to San Francisco to attend to my life there—*and* get a break. While I was away, John asked *me* to be his guardian. A sinking feeling informed me to say no, which I ultimately did. I later determined if I had agreed, I'd lose the right to be able to walk out of his room if I needed to.

In fact, twice I had to leave abruptly. Once, while in his room, I sat in a chair facing him and the door. I had placed my purse down on the floor. The topic of conversation wasn't memorable, but within a moment I *clearly* sensed *with urgency* a need to grab my purse and leave. I couldn't say why. But in a rare occurrence, I pushed past my own intuition and stayed. Within a minute or so, that feeling returned even stronger. This time I knew I had to respond. Without a word, I reached down for my purse, grabbed it, and headed for the door—all as John was starting a sentence. He abruptly stopped.

> *Without a word, I reached down for my purse, grabbed it, and headed for the door—all as John was starting a sentence. He abruptly stopped.*

"Don't go, wait," he said. Whatever he was about to say was causing me to react. I knew it. So, over his objections, I left, never knowing what he was about to say. I simply sensed a need to leave and did it. The next time I felt the same urgency to pick up my purse and leave fast, I did so without hesitation. In both cases, I honored my intuition. That felt absolutely right.

John and the Guardian Story

John Griebel officially became John's guardian on May 21st. Days later, he visited with my brother for more than an hour. But that wasn't their first meeting. In the 1970s, a tenant in one of the apartments we owned had taken a shotgun to his head. Newly divorced. Deeply unhappy. John had found the dead tenant and because there were no cleanup companies to hire, he had to clean up the mess himself. All of it.

As the county's new coroner at the time, John Griebel had come to investigate the death and met both Mom and John that day. He remained as coroner for all these years while doing guardianship work on the side. Did he and my brother ever speak about that suicide? I don't know. But how astonishing that the coroner from that time still had a role in our family.

The last week of John's life was hard.

John held hands with his guardian as they spoke, my brother in bed with John Griebel standing next to it. I sat at the foot of the bed and watched this extraordinary moment unfold. It was almost like watching John talking to Dad. Our dad and the coroner were similar in physique and manner, and especially in their manner. My brother spoke almost the entire time. The best he could, he apologized for all he'd said in the past while John Griebel had been guardian for Mom. John shared details I had not heard before—such as the feelings he experienced every time he walked into the empty log cabin. He said it was awful. The silence. The loneliness. Knowing no one else was there. Just him.

I heard him choke up and saw him cry—for the first (and only) time. I suspect this time was deeply cleansing for my brother.

When I had visited John on Wednesday, June 5th, we agreed I should call the next day to find out if he wanted me to come again. His time was getting close. When I called Thursday at the designated time, the nurse took the hall phone to his room and said, "John, your sister's on the phone." She had to ask him several times if he wanted me to come see him. I could hear his shallow voice say, "No." It was hard for me to hear that answer, but I knew. I had no need to see him one more time. He didn't either. It was over.

At the End

My brother had been at the care center a little over two months when he passed, alone, at dawn on Friday, June 7, 2013. Hospice had been involved during his final weeks. It seems he died on his own terms. If John had wanted someone there, he would have asked for it.

I had told John Griebel I wanted to be there when John passed if possible, but he strongly recommended I *not* be present. "Based on my experience as coroner, that is what you'll remember," he said, referring to the gruesomeness of death.

The morning my brother passed, I saw a beautiful dawn emerging from my Lake Geneva apartment window—stunning pink with blue clouds. Unusual. It felt like a sign. Then the call came from John Griebel. He asked if I wanted to see John's body, that he would meet me at the care center. "Yes, I'm on my way," I said. Then I called my children and also Lynn, who said he wanted to come as well.

It felt strange seeing my brother's body, but deep inside, I knew I should for two reasons. It was like being at an airport seeing a loved one depart. Yes, I did want to see him off. But I had another reason, a different one. *I had to know he was really gone.*

In disbelief, I stood there feeling torn between sadness and relief. This was just surreal.

As I looked around the room with him still lying there, his blue eyes open, I felt sad. But I also wondered what took him so long to go, given that his mother had died eight years earlier.

I picked up his briefcase and opened it. His wallet was there. His tape recorder, too. And his glasses. All so personal. It was over. Really over.

Memories about John? They are few. He and I had lived separate childhoods and had different experiences with our parents. The black Labrador retriever was his, the jeep vehicle was his, the brand-new Ford Mustang was his. Planting corn one summer in the 11 acres across the street using our tractor, plow, and disc—that was all his. I used to ride along to help him plant the corn, sitting on the side of the tractor while he drove. On occasion, I went with him when he mowed lawns for people.

After Dad died, John and I both wanted to learn to water ski. Doing that became one of our best moments. So was his taking me to see Barbra Streisand perform at Chicago's Soldier's Field. John knew I loved her music.

Sadly, there wasn't much between us except these few memories. That was something, at least.

His Funeral Story

Where could we have a funeral service? No church pastors were willing to step up and claim John as one of their own. All requests were met with silence. I was threading a needle. What was right for the one who passed versus those still alive and wanting to say goodbye? The answer was to have no church service at all.

Instead, we had a short visitation at the same funeral home we went to for Dad's service in 1965. Then we had a gravesite service led by a minister recommended by the funeral home, all on Friday afternoon before the Labor Day weekend. That felt right.

Delaying the service for three months after his death was necessary so we could have a marker made. It was designed by my daughter and placed close to Dad's stone that straddles two plots. John's marker was centered on one of the plots.

Right after Dad died, I remember John telling me he wanted to step into Dad's shoes. It seemed sad yet poignant that his wake was held at the same place as Dad's, that John's ashes were buried next to Dad's—a father now watching over his son. Ironically, back in 1965, John and I had selected the plots together near the beautiful oak trees, a lovely and peaceful site.

I had sensed the right people would come to John's funeral. And they did—about 30 of them—both high school classmates and more recent friends. Some I knew; others I didn't. My college roommate came (she knew John, too). My ex-husband came. My kids and I were present. One of our cousins came all the way from Norway. John's attorney attended. So did Lynn, John Griebel, and others—some even on their lunch break from work. Just the fact that they came told me they cared.

However, when you don't know all that's going on in a person's life, I guess it would have been tough for anyone to step in and ask, "Can I help you?" Especially when Mom and John had been so secretive. She taught him that. He was open and friendly by nature, but Mom had controlled him for decades.

John at 19 with Dad and Mom's Chevy Impala Oct 1963.

Resolving John's estate took about two years. It closed exactly 50 years after Dad had died and with it came emotional closure for me. Our whole family had been stuck in time over what had happened in 1965.

Finding John's assets was easy, yet messy, too. He had done his own taxes all these years—by hand. However, lots of his assets had reverted to the state of Wisconsin because managing them just got away from him. He never did change his 1975 will; he died leaving it all to Mom and her heirs. I was the only one left.

3

My Family House—The Log Cabin

Growing up, this was my home.

MY CHILDHOOD HOME LOOKED AWFUL. I HAD DRIVEN by earlier before I was able to get in. There were no lights on. With all the dead trees out front, the place looked eerie. Creepy eerie.

I had hired Lynn Fischer and a friend, Karen, to help me deal with the immense work the house would require. As we walked in, it felt like the first step was to rescue the old treasures and memories.

We started in the living room removing what valuables we

could find. I had anticipated we'd face a possible security risk and, to store everything we found, I had secured a storage facility nearby. Anything of serious worth we'd place in a safe deposit box. That was the plan.

I sensed to go clockwise around the room, although it seemed odd for my approach to be so methodical. What was there wasn't valuable, just important to me emotionally. My heart wanted to secure a particular china set in a built-in open hutch. Mom had found this dinnerware—hand painted Noritake "M" from Japan—at a garage sale years before. Our family just used the dessert plates and only for serving birthday cakes from a favorite local bakery. I wanted to retrieve at least one of those plates.

We found little plastic sandwich baggies filled with loose change in various places where Mom had hidden them. Not a lot—just pennies and a few nickels and dimes. Weird she would do that. It might be just how she dealt with her loose change—by making it harder for anyone (like John) to steal if it were in one place.

On the fireplace mantel was the clock that had kept time accurately all the years I lived there. Not anymore. Picking up the old clock, I noticed a photo on the mantel under it. John's high school graduation photo—placed face down. I suspect Mom did that, perhaps something to do with protecting him. Or possibly she wished that time would stand still for him, ensuring he'd never leave.

Lynn climbed from the balcony to the open top of the living room closet where a mounted stuffed squirrel kept watch over the living room along with one pheasant and two deer heads.

There, he found an envelope with cash in it. In her handwriting, sometime in the late '80s, Mom had written on it "for Johnny," and also wrote, "but he says he doesn't want it."

The entire time we spent searching the living room, I sensed we were not to go into the porch area. Something or someone was directing this search energetically. "Methodical" was the overall feeling I had. Even though I had a question that still needed resolving, we stayed in the living room as the search itself seemed to require.

> *Something or someone was directing this search energetically. "Methodical" was the overall feeling I had.*

Mom's Gift of a Diamond Ring

Also in the late 1980s, Mom had given me—with no fanfare, sentiment, or instructions—a diamond ring her father Jacob had worn. That's when she told me she'd hidden her other jewelry under the floorboards in the living room. This suggested something was wrong between her and John. But she didn't say what. And I didn't ask. I simply accepted the ring.

Why didn't Mom give the ring to John? I suspect my return to the Lake Geneva area raised issues between them that had never been addressed. She'd always been able to control him, but in the late 1980s, that balance of power was beginning to shift. Twenty-five years later, were the stashed jewelry items still there?

Mom's Jewelry Under the Living Room Floorboards Story

When Mom told me she'd hidden her jewelry in the living room under the floorboards, she indicated she put it inside one of the cold air return vents. The three of us located the vent by the stairs that went up to the balcony as well as two of the bedrooms and the bathroom. *Was her jewelry still there, or had John found it?*

To reach into the vent, we had to move the concrete blocks partially covering it. Years before, John had stacked them at the bottom of the stairs. Then Lynn took his flashlight and looked into the vent. "Plastic. I see plastic," he said and pulled out several clear plastic bags.

Inside the bags were Mom's diamond wedding rings, a diamond watch Dad had given her, and jewelry I hadn't seen before. Some items that seemed inexpensive had been purchased after Dad's death. But one piece was a pair of earrings with tiny emeralds that were understated like the real her—subdued, no flash, no calling attention to herself. She didn't *want* to look like she had money.

We also found two small boxes she apparently cherished. On the bottom of the bigger of the two boxes was a note that read: *Jan. 16, 1980 This box came from Africa 1944—silver and teakwood or mahogany—as a gift to me! E B Syver*

In a plastic bag near the boxes, we found two potholders— one bright red and the other bright yellow. With the potholders,

I found a photograph of Mom and her best childhood friend as adults. They were both smiling as if they were overjoyed that we'd found this stash. Surreal.

Seeing Mom's watch and her wedding rings hit me hard with a deep sense of familiarity—of something that had been lost to me for a long time. She was the person who taught me how to write my name, my ABCs, and my numbers. She also taught me how to swim and ride a bike.

For me, the rings and watch represented the mother I knew—the good one. Feelings of longing to see her again resonated from my heart.

I had retrieved the dinnerware set *and* my answer to whether Mom's jewelry was still there. That felt good. Then we worked through the rest of the living room, knowing we'd search the other rooms on the days that followed.

Two necessary searches stuck out in my mind—the safe in the basement and Dad's office. I knew where the safe was—by the furnace where it had always been and covered with a cloth. John had leaned an outboard boat motor against it, likely to deter someone from looking there. *Where was the combination?* Then I went upstairs to the kitchen. I had a feeling to do that.

Breaking into the Family Safe Story

While I stood at the kitchen sink near the windows and thought about the combination, I sensed this message: *You know more than you think you do.*

Huh? I wondered.

Then my head slowly turned toward the wall above the kitchen trash can. A wooden knick-knack shelf had been hanging on that wall for years. I saw miscellaneous items on it, including two white index cards. On one was written the grace we said every Sunday at our family dinner, and on the other was the combination to the safe! *Just where Mom had always kept it. John had never moved it.*

I shouted for Karen to help me, and we headed downstairs to the basement. It felt like I was breaking into my own family's safe. As I read Mom's handwriting on the index card while working the dial on the safe, I remembered having turned that dial before. Sometime after Dad had died, Mom showed me how to do this, but I'd forgotten all about it.

I turned the dial carefully one way and then the other. I reached for the handle. *Would it open? Was there anything inside?* Click! The contents were still intact: Old coins (gold ones) Dad had collected. Titles to vehicles we had owned. Quarters. Lots of quarters. Dimes. And small bars of silver.

The next day, I moved the contents into a safe deposit box at a nearby bank. Still, I felt strange going into Dad's safe as if I weren't supposed to unless there was a family emergency.

This was an emergency.

Then there was Dad's office.

Dad's Office Story

Dad's first office was in the log cabin. Later, he set up an office in Syverstad, the subdivision he created in Lake Geneva. After Dad died, Mom and John closed the Syverstad office and made the subdivision office/house a rental property. This first office still had Dad's desk, office chair, old file cabinets, a sitting bench, and original items such as a small glass container for paperclips. All were still there.

Dad's business files from 1965 remained in the file cabinets. Seeing his handwriting on them brought me back in time. So did noticing all the now-useless rental property keys that still hung on the back of the office door.

This had been John's office space, a place where we couldn't put our feet anywhere without stepping on papers. Sensitive documents and bank statements were lying out in the open for anyone to see. So were his personal tax records. And lots of mail, most of it unopened.

Around the room, we noticed precious old items: Dad's Polaroid camera, his survey equipment, and a movie projector with a large pull-up screen for watching the movies he'd taken of us. So many memories dwelled in this one room—mixed with the stark reality of what had occurred since.

We gathered the papers, documents, tax files, Dad's business files, and stock certificates. Some certificates dated back to the 1960s and were filed in an unlocked bottom file drawer. Plus we found Dad's immigration and naturalization documents.

As I stood shoving files into black garbage bags, I looked up. On top of the cabinet, I saw the place where Dad always kept his Hershey chocolate bars—the ones I used to sneak before I became allergic to chocolate.

John's Bedroom Story

John had taken over my bedroom years before, likely because it was next to the bathroom and was warmer than his room on the porch. There, the heat came up from the living room.

In an odd sort of a way, I want to talk about John's bedroom on the porch. It's where he had to move when I came along as a newborn. For years, John occupied a room of his own there with a door that locked. Then when Mom moved out of Dad's room, she made the large open part of the porch her bedroom. That happened when John was about 12.

We stepped into my former bedroom, John's bedroom upstairs above the kitchen. Just like when I visited in 2006, I saw my high school and college memorabilia on the wall in the same place. Same furniture. Same bed. Lots of clutter. And like in the office downstairs, it was hard to put a foot down without stepping on something.

I looked around. *What did I want to rescue from this space?*

My Augustana College mug. That's where I had started my college career. So, I took the mug.

Clearing the rest could wait. However, red flags of disgust and warning of trouble were going off. We found audio tapes of probably every conversation he'd ever had in recent years—both telephone and in person. Surprisingly, the cassette tapes were neatly coded with initials and letters showing some degree of organization. I suspect he wanted to capture what people would say so he could hold them to it. We later burned them all.

Discovering the tapes—that's when I recalled John trying to record the judge at the court hearing for Mom's estate in 2005. The bailiff had leaned over and told the judge about it. He then spoke directly to John who acknowledged he was recording the hearings. The judge told him to stop, which he did.

In the rest of the house, mice had free reign feasting on half-eaten cartons of food. Lynn found mice feces and nests everywhere, including in the closets. John had excessively kept things in case he'd ever need them—something I suspect he learned from Mom, a depression-era kid. My brother cut his own hair and even kept a bag full of trimmings in the basement—along with locks, keys, padlocks, and a lot more.

No Room for Individuality
Because of Mom, this became a house of obedience for John. Authoritarians do that to you. They expect you to shut down, to be not yourself but instead to fall in line with what is

demanded. That's how my mother behaved. I suspect her own mother did, too.

The way Mom grew up, there was no room for individuality. No room for self-expression. Any backtalk elicited a "shut up" or "silence!" John likely got some of this treatment, too, and he had been put on a short leash at a young age—a leash she never took off.

I routinely progressed with my search for family assets but also sensed not to enter this room or that room. My hesitation reflected my belief that everyone needs a safe environment—and a feeling of being safe from within. Both kinds of "safe."

My hesitation reflected my belief that everyone needs a safe environment—and a feeling of being safe from within. Both kinds of "safe."

After all, the house you grew up in holds a special place in your life. It just does. So do the people in your world at that time—for good or bad. Writing this chapter allowed me to say goodbye to my childhood home, to the people in them, and to what went on inside its walls.

Is there someone or something you know deep down that you need to say goodbye to?

A Cookbook and Holidays Remembered

For the sake of *good* memories, I wanted to find Mom's cookbook from the 1940s. It was a *Good Housekeeping* cookbook with a green insert about rationing food, as people did during the war years. Mom and I didn't cook or bake together, but I still wanted this treasured cookbook just because it was hers. We looked everywhere it should have been—to no avail.

I will always remember the Thanksgivings, birthdays, and Christmases celebrated in that house—usually with only the four of us. No one else came. For Thanksgiving, Mom cooked the turkey with all the fixings and baked a pumpkin chiffon pie. For birthdays, we had cake served on those memorable plates I retrieved from the living room hutch.

Christmases were special, too. We had a tall tree in the living room. Lots of lights, ornaments, and tinsel. Presents under the tree. Another turkey dinner. Again, just the four of us.

The Eve of St. Nicholas, the night before December 6th, was a big deal for Mom, who grew up with this Austrian holiday tradition. Once we were old enough, John would walk me down Linn Road to the next street and then come back through the lumberyard to the house. First, we had to see if the candle Mom had lit on the mantel before we left had gone out. If yes, then we knew St. Nick had come. That meant we could come back in and find a simple present such as a new coloring book with a box of crayons.

Suspended from the ceiling of our house was an oxen yoke with two lanterns built into it. We rarely used the lamps, only because the wall light switch for it had shorted out years earlier, but this feature was unique. Our house was also different because it had dragons on the roofline, built by our Norwegian dad. He had mounted three large spotlights at the peaks of the roof, and we called those spotlights "beacons."

This was the house Dad built—and it's where we lost him.

My Childhood Home Taken Apart

Before we tore down the log cabin, my childhood home, I had architectural record drawings made and professional photographs taken. To this day, I own the land. The house and remaining structures had to go.

Gradually, the house was cleaned out and manually taken apart. We had to use dumpsters, recycling bins, municipal trash cans, and a burn site. We recycled everything we could, landfilled only what had to be, and burned the rest—like a cremation. That process took a full year, although it wasn't until 2017 that the basement and the Chevy garage were excavated. Since then, the land has been cleared and restored for future use.

Although I won't miss the log cabin and all the negativity it represents, the land where it stood continues to heal me. At some point, it too will have to go as I move on.

The log cabin being cleared away.

4

A Revealing Diary Hidden from View

*Matters we throw under the proverbial rug
instead of openly processing them can have
profound effects on others around you.*

At John's funeral, Lynn Fischer walked up to me and expressed his condolences as he had several times before. Then he said, "I found something in the house. You have to see it." He didn't have it with him. I thought he might have found Mom's cookbook—the one I had been wondering about.

Mom's Hidden Diary Found Story

Wednesday, September 4th, five days after John's funeral, I was able to get back to the log cabin. I parked my rental car in Mom's driveway and walked across the grass to the living room door, which was wide open. Lynn was inside working. I announced myself without going inside. I just couldn't go in. Too many memories.

As Lynn walked across the living room, I saw he had something in his hand. No, not Mom's cookbook—something even better. A handwritten diary she had kept that referenced events in 1960, 1961, and 1962. I didn't know it existed. I don't believe *anyone* did, except Mom.

When I saw this red spiralbound notebook, even from a distance, I knew: THIS IS A GIFT. One that would make a difference.

Lynn and Mom had been close in a few ways. They shared the same birthday, November 14th. On occasion, she'd visit and drink beer with him. And when she had trouble with John, she often turned to Lynn for help. It may have been important I hired him to take apart the house. Then "she" could direct him to find the diary.

Lynn told me every time he went to the porch to clean out the junk, he kept stepping on a bump in the carpet. Because of all the clutter, it took a while to get to the bump. He'd have to find the carpet's edge and pull it back to see what it might be. Finally, he did. Once he moved the oval throw rug and pulled back the carpet itself, he saw the red notebook lying on the carpet pad.

I found the following six diary entries particularly telling. I gave each of them a brief title and, because details matter, I have changed none of the wording in the excerpts themselves. For that reason, you can hear my mother's voice.

This was her voice and her reality.

"Get out," he said.

April 26th Thursday, 1962

I tried Syverstad door at 1 pm today—and John had changed the lock someway so I could not use my key. So, I banged hard on the screen—and demanded to be let in.—

Finally Syver came to the door and tried to <u>push me out</u>—but I pushed right past him. (He glanced over and saw that [our two employees] were there and would have a witness) and so he let me pass.

Later I asked him for the key to the door and he said, "I won't get one" and "get out"—I told him it is my house, too, and my money in that house and I will stay and come and go any way I want as I've always done.

Then he called Mr. C. [his attorney] and told him I am annoying him and wondered how he could stop me, that I almost punched in the window screen—(Before this, John said he would get an injunction restraining me from being in Syverstad.)

Our pistol went missing.

April 26th Thursday, 1962

Tonight at 5:30 John came in when I was gone and Mariane said dad went upstairs to a closet—one which he never usually goes to—and walked out a couple of minutes later. I checked the closet and the pistol was gone.

It had been there on Monday as I cleaned the closet and it was on the very top part of it.—And Mr. S. [John] was in, she [Mariane] said, just for a couple of minutes and left.

I called Mr. C. [his attorney] and he said, "That's real bad. I'll try and find him and get it away from him."

I called Mr. B.'s [insurance agent] home and asked Mrs. B. to tell Johnny, Jr. to call me before he left there—as he is driving my yellow Chevy and I wouldn't want him to stop in Syverstad and have his Dad mistake him for me and shoot him.

9 pm—Mr. C. arrived here and said he cannot find Syver any place because he went to Syverstad—he went to Wooddale—and cannot locate him.

He said for me not to leave here or go near Syverstad.

Later 9:15—Mr. R. [also his attorney] called and I told him about the missing gun.

9:30 pm Johnny called and I warned him not to go near Syverstad as dad has the pistol and he might mistake him for me and kill him as Dad is vicious now.

Besides Johnny has my yellow car—

Lies and more lies.

April 27th, 1962

Friday morning 8:30. John came to breakfast as always—He arrived home 10:30 pm last night and he talked about the Stone Manor, etc.

I asked him where he went last night. He said, "Toastmaster Club." But he said he did not stay long.

Then I asked him why he came home at 5:30 [the previous evening], as I was not home.

He said to get a clean shirt and make some phone calls.

I asked him then if he knew what became of the pistol that was in the closet upstairs. He calmly replied, "No, isn't it there?" I said, "No, that you came back to get the shirt and also the gun." He did not deny it or agree.

Dad's relations with Mrs. H.

April 27th, 1962

I told John that I warned Johnny not to go near Syverstad as it is pitch dark at the house even though street lights are there and he may be mistaken for me—and with John's desperation in being trapped and exposed—with his relations with Mrs. H. [a lady friend]—and, knowing that I object to it—he by shooting me (accidentally or as a prowler) he would get by easily and then he wouldn't have to be concerned about getting my signature on any more mortgages (which signature he needs) and, of course, then he would be free to have

Mrs. H. at Syverstad with him in the temporary office with no interference from me. [Note: the bank insisted John's wife co-sign for mortgages because of John's poor health.]

A skirt-chaser. And violent. My dad—really?

May 8th, 1962 and May 9th, 1962

I said that in view of the fact that he had 3 women (seriously to the detriment of family and business life for 2 years)—and has locked me out of Syverstad—this time Mrs. H. is the cause—and also Mrs. P. and 3 girls—teen age last July—(61)—whom he had fooled around with for 4 days—and this time when Mrs. T. [a family friend] and I were at Syverstad, he had 3 girls in the front seat of the boat all over Lk Geneva until later than 10 pm—That time he was violent, too, when I demanded an explanation—because I heard him tell them that he would see them [the 3 girls] or her [Mrs. P.] tomorrow again—One seemed more aggressive and ugly toward me when I asked what they were doing with my husband at that late hour—They ran—up the hill—.

A long time afterward he was intense upon visiting one of the girls in Chicago—he even said he'd take one [of] the children with him—I said that he better not dare, as they [Johnny and Mariane] are minor children—and I'd see to it that they would not be subjected to such indignities by their father—

So it appears that at his age—58-59-60 he is a skirt chaser—

"Dark Hole" and a Christmas drunk. "Get your stuff and get out."

In November 14, 1961 (under John and Mr. C's diabolical threats) I signed $21,000 mortgage on L11—Syverstad—John was less than $1,000 in cash—because of his playboy ways with Mrs. P.—in Syverstad for two years—During these times he called [our] log cabin homestead a "Dark Hole" and he acted as though he hated all 3 of us [Mariane, Johnny, and me]—Some nights—many nights—he did not arrive home until 10:30 or 11 or later at night—some nights did not come home at all—

Christmas '61—he was a terrible friend—drunk—(I think) and held us at bay [on] Christmas Eve—until Johnny could hardly talk and breathe—Mariane was stunned and I asked him at 10 pm to get his stuff and get out. He stayed—and was terrible—until 11:30 pm.

(End of Diary excerpts)

My initial response to Mom's diary: I knew all the names and episodes she wrote about when they occurred. Mom had told me about some of them and others I had witnessed myself. I felt this was *their* issue, not mine. As to this last excerpt about Christmas 1961, I remember it clearly. I wasn't stunned. I was distanced. I recall her yelling at Dad something about all the land we owned and how "you can't eat dirt." Mom was worried about money.

That night, I remember walking upstairs to my room and going to bed. Eventually, so did everyone else. Then I snuck downstairs and pulled out my Christmas gifts from under the tree. I carried them up to my bedroom and went under my bed. With a flashlight in my hand, I opened my presents. I already knew what each was; I had peeked while they were under the tree. The gifts did not disappoint me. My parents did.

The cover of Mom's diary

Illuminating Answers

What Mom wrote answered many questions for me—including why I had the epiphany I did at the age of 12/13. *Something was wrong in the house. I didn't know what it was, I just knew it wasn't me.* That realization happened sometime during the exact years Mom referenced in her diary.

What I *didn't* know was that in the fall of 1961, Mom and Dad had both "lawyered up" to work out a divorce settlement. In the spring of 1962, when most of these excerpts occurred, the paperwork was just waiting for one of them to pull the trigger.

From the diary, I also learned the situation was dangerously bad for Mom and possibly for John, too. Clearly, the people in our house didn't feel safe. It wasn't just me.

In June 1962, Mom wrote about an incident that pushed her to call her attorney and say she was done. Dad was notified of this by his attorney. However, nothing happened. He had packed his belongings and was ready to leave the log cabin when they began talking a bit more. Again, nothing advanced.

Then one night almost three years to the day, Dad died.

During those three years, John had gone off to an out-of-state college, so it was just Dad, Mom, and me at home. Looking back, the threat of their languishing divorce was palpable during each of my high school freshman, sophomore, and junior years. It was awful. I felt I began my freshman year without any parents. As told in the story "Suicide Thoughts at Age Fifteen" in Book 1, as a sophomore, I stood in front of the bathroom sink one morning when an involuntary thought of death came forth on its own. I didn't know why. I retell that story here.

Suicide Thoughts at Age Fifteen (Revisited)

When I was 15 years old and a sophomore in high school, I experienced thoughts of suicide. But they weren't the "normal" kind. They came from an "involuntary place" within me.

Here's what happened. One morning, I was getting ready for school as usual. I stood in the bathroom in front of the sink grooming my eyebrows with a single-edge razor blade (because I didn't know I was supposed to pluck them using tweezers). At some point, I found myself looking down at the blade in my right hand. Suddenly, my eyes seemed to have a mind of their own. My gaze moved over to the inside of my left wrist, and I had the thought this would be so easy.

It scared the bejeebers out of me.

Where did that come from? I quickly sat down on the side of the bathtub and paused. What just happened? I didn't call out for help. I didn't go to Mom or Dad. I just sat for a bit. Then I decided I wasn't going to school that day.

Next, I opened the bathroom door, walked out onto the balcony over the living room, saw Mom below, and calmly said to her, "I don't feel well, and I'm not going to school today." Then I said, "I think I want to talk with our minister." She looked at me and didn't say anything or ask questions. Finally, she said, "Okay."

My minister was at the Lutheran Church in Lake Geneva. I didn't know him very well, but something inside told me he was the person to call. I called the church that morning and asked if he was available. He would be later in the afternoon, I learned, so I made an appointment.

Psychological counseling had a stigma to it back then, so seeing that kind of counselor wasn't an option. Also, in my world, there were few people I could have talked to about this whom Mom would have approved of. In fact, the reverend was the only one. That afternoon, he and I talked for a while, although I had no words to describe my experience to him. All in all, he didn't do much, but talking with him was something.

Although he didn't know me well at all, he knew who I was. His approach was to first ask me to get a transcript from my school so he could see my academic record. It took a few days to get the transcript, but when I showed it to him, he was pleasantly surprised at how well I was doing academically. However, he said I needed to cut back on all my extra-curricular activities. That was about the time one of my teachers was encouraging me to join forensics—one more extra-curricular activity. So based on the reverend's advice, I backed off the forensics. But I noticed that less activity did seem to ease whatever was going on. Part of me apparently wanted "out."

It would be slightly more than a year later when Dad would pass. Then things actually got worse.

Luckily, I had reached for help outside my family. That relieved some of the pressure I was under—but only some of it. And the stories you'll read about the Log Cabin Girl and the Office Girl when I was a junior describe events of the heart I never got over.

It Really Wasn't Me . . . It Was Them

Seeing and reading Mom's diary for the first time in 2013 gave me answers I didn't have. Knowing their divorce was imminent helped me see the trouble wasn't *me*; it was *them*. The diary made me remember all the things I knew back then and recall now. It confirms how I distanced myself to survive their issues. Again, these issues, as awful as they could be, were not mine. And if they had divorced, perhaps Dad wouldn't have died when he did. It was his death that made everything in my world so much worse.

Mainly, the diary unveiled trouble in our family—in many forms. Trouble with the properties and property lawsuits. Trouble with Dad's Syverstad house where he had an office. Trouble with his health after his first heart attack in 1957. And trouble in their marriage. All those details noted in Mom's diary led to Dad calling our house, the log cabin, "the Dark Hole." I suspect Mom wrote them to make sure *someone* knew. She wanted a witness, although she kept this diary a secret the rest of her life. Her entries confirmed what I already knew, written in a familiar way about familiar people. Mostly, it spoke volumes about the strain in their marriage.

But if I had known divorce terms were on the table, I might have looked at my parents differently. And that might have changed my next 50 years. My knowing about a possible divorce would have at least validated the truth of my epiphany—that there was *something wrong in the house.*

What kinds of secrets were in your family as you grew up?

5

The Presence of Negative Energy

What I didn't know, mattered.

Sometime during the first two years after Mom died, I began hearing details from a few of her friends. The basic story was that Dad met Mom while he was still married to his first wife.

She had been working in a clothing store. He walked into the store one day, and she later told me she liked his accent. The story goes that he hired her as a housekeeper. It didn't take long after that for his wife of 10 years to leave him. A divorce settlement and a lot of indignation followed. He and his first wife had no children.

Mom and Dad married in 1942, a little over a year after his divorce was final. When Mom and Dad's pending divorce stalled in 1962, they had been married for 20 years.

The First Wife's Energy Story

During the early years of Mom's estate settlement, I found myself exploring parts of the house in my mind's eye. Even as a kid, an area in the basement back by the furnace kept drawing my attention. It always felt creepy—really creepy.

Many years later as I "looked" in that basement area, it still felt creepy—like something was there. *There was.* I thought I should have run, but I stood my ground. I was curious. Gradually I "saw" two red eyes moving toward me. I "saw" it had a form. As I watched it come closer, I could tell it was a human form—the form of a woman. Her eyes were red with anger, embarrassment, and shame. I knew who it was—the energy of the first wife.

I told her I knew who she was, and that she couldn't stay here. No response.

After several encounters, finally she said she would go. In the days that followed, I told others what I'd learned about Dad's divorcing his first wife. I empathized how it must have felt for her to end her marriage this way. But I did not share the part about "seeing" her in the basement.

Sometime later, my attention was drawn to the basement again. I sensed a truck was backing down Dad's driveway. In my mind, I stood by the open garage doors as the truck pulled up in front of them. Then I "saw" her walk from the furnace area and go past me to the truck and get in it. "Good for her," I thought. "She needed to leave." Then I "heard" the truck drive away.

A while later, while sitting in my bed journaling, I heard someone "sitting" next to me say directly into my left ear, "THANK YOU." I jumped but only slightly as I instantly realized who it was. *The first wife.* It *felt* like her.

Apparently, all the words spoken about her had made a difference for her energetically. It told me that energy can heal.

Writing about it can also heal.

John's Trauma Story

Living with Mom, my brother lost out when it came to certain issues between Mom and Dad. One centered around Mom's favoring her son and making him a mama's boy over Dad's objections. After Dad died, my brother had to deal with Mom while trying to step into his father's shoes—not easy.

In addition to our father's death, John experienced four other tragic events that left their own traumatic marks. One was a fatal boating accident that involved John, but it wasn't his fault. Another was a friend dying in an airplane crash. Then an attorney friend died in a private plane crash. John planned to be on board that plane, but at the last minute he chose to drive with Mom instead. And he had to deal with the suicide at the apartment.

I don't think he ever got over any of it.

Mom's Energy Story

Mom came into her marriage with a lot of issues. She'd had an abusive childhood at the hand of her authoritarian mother and had experienced the early death of her father. She dropped out of high school. I *suspect* she had depression, but I *know* she had secrets. She once said she was born under the sign of Scorpio and that Scorpios are known for keeping secrets. She also told me she liked her secrets.

Mom was a fraction of who she could have been.

In *Abuse & Energy*, I wrote that Mom told me she had a black cloud over her head for years. She didn't know how it got there. Once she became bedridden at the log cabin, that black cloud left. What was it? Why did it leave? I suspect the black cloud was unprocessed grief about her dad's death and sadness, perhaps regret, too, that she had never finished school or fulfilled her potential. It also seemed like trouble followed Mom. I believe that black cloud left because she was done. She was living out her exit plan.

What might you regret that you still have the power to change?

Dark Energy at the Apartments Story

Mom's estate included rental apartments that had been in the family for years. Not well maintained, the apartments were almost all empty by the time she passed.

These apartments had been owned by Dad, but the year before he died, he sold them. As fate would have it, a year after he died, the owner defaulted on payments, so the property came back into the estate and became part of their business.

Whenever I visited these apartments, I got a creepy feeling. There was such negative energy in that place. It could have originated with anyone—a tenant, a buoy renter, or even a visitor. Sometimes, I think that Dad or John may have brought it home with them to the log cabin.

Mom's Cookbook Mysteriously Found Story

Mom's cookbook, her *Good Housekeeping* one from the 1940s, had gone missing. We couldn't locate it anywhere during our initial search. Eventually, Lynn found it in the house. Someone had opened the cookbook to the middle page, bent the covers all the way back, then tied it inside out with thick rope, mangling its spine. It was the kind of rope that John had used at the apartments. I shivered when I saw it.

Black Flies Surrounding Mom's Buick Story

After Mom died in 2005, John began driving her Buick. When I got to the house, he had backed it into the garage so the car would face outward. The garage door had deteriorated so much, it wouldn't close, so it had been left wide open—for years.

Because of dealing with everything inside the house, it took me an agonizingly long while to get to the matter of the Buick. When I finally did, I sensed I'd feel a kind of relief. And I did.

John had backed it into the garage but not all the way. As a result, I had to walk up to the front grille with its headlights facing me *as if John were watching*. It felt intimidating. Added to that were the large black flies all over her car. Oddly, they weren't anywhere else in the garage or outside of it. Dozens of them swarmed the car.

Lynn and I had looked everywhere in the house and in obvious places in the garage for the key to the Buick. Finally, we found it on one of the rafters in the garage. Lynn had to stand on the back bumper of the car to reach it.

Once we opened the car doors with the key, we looked into the trunk loaded with many of Mom's belongings. Her golf clubs. A packed suitcase. Her purse. (It felt eerie to open her purse, find her wallet, and see her driver's license.) And a box. *All of these items had been in the trunk ever since she died eight years before.*

At our mother's gravesite, John had requested that I give him some of her ashes to spread. I saw they were still in the box I'd handed him in 2005. He had never spread them; he'd just left them in the trunk.

It seemed dark negative energy prevailed everywhere in the log cabin. Was it the anger of Dad's first wife? Was it Mom's own abusive childhood or her father's death early in life? Was it about the secrets Mom kept? Was it the reason she purchased two cottages, one in northern Wisconsin and the other in Florida? Mom did not invite me, my husband, our kids, or John to either place, yet she owned them for years. Was her secrecy related to John and all his traumas? And what did the black flies around Mom's car indicate?

Low-vibration Energy

With low-vibration anger emanating from the basement of the house where a second wife and two children were living, how can there *not* be an effect? This kind of energy—the low-vibration kind—shows up as anger, shame, hatred, jealousy, depression, secrets, dismissiveness. And it invites other dark energies to join in.

Negative energy likely began in our house as early as 1940—energy that remained until John died and the house was demolished in 2014. We'll never know exactly what effects this dark energy had on its four occupants. But negative energy is what I was reacting to. I *sense* energy. And I think others do, too.

6

When Negative Energy Leaves

It's the darkest before the dawn.

THIS BOOK AND SERIES HAVE HELPED ME UNDERSTAND the intuitive Flashlight I've used to find my way as a child and an adult.

I have experienced an internal energy fight during which I realized the more I trusted myself, the more I journaled and meditated. The more I journaled, the more of the real me came forth. The more I meditated, the same. The more I actually wrote, even more of me came forth. This effort brought out such physical responses as cold feet, cold spots around my body, dry mouth, gradually increased heartbeat, and digestive problems, to name a few. Collectively, these responses marked a turning point. I discovered that when old energy is released, it frees up space within our bodies for our own true energy to fill in.

The truth is, the firing up of my own energy—through journaling, meditation, counseling, and writing—slowly but surely pushed out the old negative energy. It was released any way it could as fast as it could. As a result, my physical discomforts generally disappeared within 10 days.

Emotional releases that lead to physical releases are about letting go of energy that never should have been allowed to build in the first place. It's energy that was never released at the time the trauma or abuse occurred—such as not grieving a loved one's death.

Old energy includes not just yours but other people's energy as well. This involves their thoughts, ideas, ideology, and way of thinking. That means people around you—anyone who offers ideas as true when they're false—can be part of the problem. And even if it is a kind of truth, it's not necessarily *your* truth. It is *their* truth. It's likely you have taken in a falsehood and made it yours.

Having massages can help release some of this energy. They allow you to open up energetically and even reclaim lost aspects of yourself. The release during the first week of January 2017, described in the story that follows, was similar to the release from my chocolate allergy in 2001. Both were major.

It started after a two-hour massage with grapeseed oil that not only produced physical effects but psychic ones, too.

The Release of Toxins and Tears Story

At first, I had a slight fever that subsided quickly. But for six days after the massage, I felt awful. Release of toxins, energy that wasn't mine, and built-up old energy made me physically sick. I lay on the sofa in my apartment from Sunday until Friday. I ate lightly. I appreciated how having the sofa in front of the Victorian window put me directly in the natural light and even sunshine.

It wasn't until Friday that I could turn back to my writing. That's when both my eyes teared up excessively. A newly elected U.S. president whom I didn't favor would be taking office later that month. The new president was an authoritarian who habitually lied with ease and practiced a "my way or the highway" mentality. *This was how my mother behaved!* This was January 2017.

Though I didn't know it then, later in the summer, I'd be moving back to the state where I grew up, where Dad died, where John succumbed to Mom's control, and where the log cabin was located. *This yanked my chain inside.* I use that expression more than figuratively, for inside, I had probably been chained for years. This stirred me enough to trigger a huge energy release. It took the form of excessive tearing, such that anyone witnessing it would have assumed I had been sobbing. My tearing eyes reminded me of an award-winning 1971 public service ad for Keep America Beautiful. It featured a Native American looking at a landscape full of litter. Poignantly, a tear runs down his face as if to say, "Something's wrong here."

Something was wrong in my universe.

With this release, the psychic effects I picked up on were electromagnetic. I sensed something was coming through the TV set, so I turned it off. What about the three cordless phones I had in various places around my apartment? I knew I had to turn off two of them, even unplug them. I kept only the one in the office, the room farthest away from my bedroom. In my bedroom, I unplugged and put away all electronics except my cell phone.

I kept seeing in my mind's eye a split screen of two events. On the left was the face of the new president; on the right was a spinning abyss of dark energy. I sensed the dark negative energy of the log cabin. I heard internally that it was dangerous. I strongly felt that if I were to get too close to that swirling energy, it would suck me in. So I stayed back. I never fell in.

A remedy came to mind that helped immensely. I'd put on the sleep mask I use when traveling. But not to cover my eyes. Instead, I placed it over my forehead where the energetic third eye is located. Immediately, the left side of the screen with the hateful face was gone—blocked out. But I continued to see the right side, so I strapped on the sleep mask and wore it 24-7 all month. It really helped.

I also called my counselor in Wisconsin, and we spoke extensively about my immediate situation. As the month progressed, I calmed down. I kept the TV off, the phones removed, the sleep mask on. All that, plus the counselling and writing, made a difference. By the end of January, I realized the TV needed to remain off. Being highly receptive, I still had to be careful what I was letting in through electronic means.

After a few highly emotional weeks, this release finally finished—except for a constant tearing in my eyes. It took four months for the left eye to finish tearing, and it's been fine ever since. However, the tearing in my right eye (my dominant side) went away gradually with my physician's help—but not until 2020.

This was one of the strongest natural purges I've experienced.

Have you ever experienced a physical symptom or symptoms that seemed to precede a profound spiritual experience? If yes, describe it.

Emotional abuse makes you vulnerable and gets you used to being controlled. I saw this pattern with John in our family living in the log cabin. And how did I react? I'd sum it up by saying I put myself into an emotional shutdown. *That's what I did to survive.* How do I know that? Because of all the things I "saw" when it began to unravel, beginning in 1984.

7

Call It By Its Name—Survival Mode

*The following events helped bring the
rest of me forth. This information can
help pave the way for you.*

There are many kinds of abuse. Physical, mental, verbal, emotional, financial, sexual, spiritual, and more. Each is an abuse of power.

When I started this series, I wrote "abuse renders war on the soul." Yes, abuse of any kind harms the soul mercilessly. It causes damage—the kind that can't be repaired without understanding it even exists. I wrote those words by feeling them. At the time, I did not know what was meant by damage. Now I do.

Soul fragmentation was perhaps the worst damage I experienced. Many fragments broke off and existed on their own, though not too far away from my physical self and the rest of my energy self. There they waited, hoping I would return to find them at a time when it was safe for them to come home. I also experienced an emotional allergy to chocolate that lasted for 47 years. That was part of many energy blockages inside my body damming up my energy flow.

I experienced the psychological numbing of dissociation as well. And there was more—all having an effect on the quality of my life over 70-plus years. Thankfully, almost all of that damage has been reversed. But without an understanding that this can occur, the damage can't be repaired or even prevented. It's been a long, intense journey toward 100 percent.

It's been a long, intense journey toward 100 percent.

Survival Mode

That's what I first called what I did to survive my *circumstances; I shut down emotionally.* But there was so much more. Given the breadth of what I know today, I've given it a name that describes what I actually did. I put myself into **Survival Mode.**

What exactly is Survival Mode? It is a reaction by your internal energy system that is designed to ensure you survive. Yet anything that is a response involving your energy system is a response of your soul. It is a reaction to anything that threatens your physical life, your safety, or the well-being of your soul. This reaction can disempower you by suppressing your energy system, which can cause lifelong problems. That means you will live another day, but you might experience long-term effects that could include trust issues (especially trusting yourself), low self-esteem, underachieving, issues of being controlled by others, a sense that something unknown and undefined holds you back, a feeling that trying anything new is out of your range and you don't know why, among others.

Peace within begins by building a new understanding of yourself and of the world. Once upon a time, mankind had to discover gravity—a force present in our lives that was affecting everything. We eventually gave it a name, studied it extensively, and learned. Energy is similar; it affects everything, too. We still have much to learn about this.

> *Peace within begins by building a new understanding of yourself and of the world.*

On an individual level, you have a Human Energy System that is responsible for your ability to imagine, create, empathize, embrace the rule of law, interpret morality and humanity, align with nature and its universal energy, and feel the way you are capable of. But when your energy is diminished, you are less of who you can be. Being in Survival Mode acts like a brake that holds you back. It can even hold you down; it does so to ensure you survive.

I had an energy problem . . . and energy was the solution. Studying, learning, and understanding energy changed everything. And it can for you, too, as you gain a deeper understanding of Survival Mode.

> *Studying, learning, and understanding energy changed everything.*

Do you remember that "look" your mom or dad could give that would stop you in your tracks? Even without words, you knew what it meant beneath the surface, and you responded. *That's energy.* So is experiencing any kind of abuse or trauma—such as being bullied, dismissed, marginalized, or made to feel like you didn't belong even when you thought you did.

Suffering the loss of a loved one is about energy, too.

Emotions are energy. So are thoughts.

Responding to our parents' voices and yielding to their desired behavior with just a look from them can seem like no big deal. It might be termed parental control—but what if it isn't? What if there's more beneath the surface that no one except YOU knows about?

It doesn't take much to cause harm to the energy self. In turn, it can cause you to shut down energetically, thus diminishing your ability to feel. It can be the one sole internal issue that troubles you when you're striving to be the person you always could have been.

Do you agree for yourself that by living in Survival Mode, you simply stop growing—and you feel less?

Your Inner Shutdown Plan

Because YOU have created your own inner shutdown plan, YOU are the only person who knows how to fix it. YOU are the one who knows what you did to protect yourself. But now, what once worked could be holding you back.

So, how do you know if you are emotionally shut down, if you are living in Survival Mode? Keep in mind, even a little shut down is too much. I didn't know I was shut down until things naturally began to change.

The questions that follow will help you to discern if you, too, have shut down emotionally. *You might already know it.* For me, numerous changes kept signaling something was wrong. I could have missed them but, luckily, I noticed the signs. I paid attention. I listened to my intuition. And I followed it. Now I know more. You will, too.

Start by reading these 13 characteristics of Survival Mode while asking yourself, "Am I like this?" or "Do I behave like this?"

1. *You never tell anyone about anything you experienced.* Have you ever behaved this way? And if you did tell, did others make you feel you were ratting on them? If so, something is wrong.
2. *You don't feel your emotions.* Shutting down your ability to feel serves in two ways. It allows you to comply with the demands being made on you, and it makes the situation less painful, survivable. Does this describe you?
3. *You don't like change.* You don't tolerate it well. You want things to stay the way they are. Even rearranging the household furniture may feel like too much.
4. *You are prone to excessive analytical thinking.* It can be a coping mechanism.
5. *You may experience anxiety,* especially *anticipatory anxiety,* stemming from your experiences.
6. *You don't like anything that's "different"* because it represents change. It's similar to #3.

7. *You avoid real success.* People see you and ask questions that you can't or won't answer about your past. Those in Survival Mode will put up countless roadblocks to prevent or delay success in their lives until they believe being successful just isn't worth it anymore. So they give up. Does this describe you?
8. *You keep your head low and maintain a low profile.* That way, you can get through life. It's similar to #3—in essence, a kind of hiding.
9. *You've been taught to be afraid to try anything new.* When you do, it feels like you are pushing a rock uphill. That makes the task seem impossible when it may not be at all. Getting started—that is, piercing the energy walls that keep you in check—is the awful part. Those walls were built to keep you in your place.
10. *Generally, you are being controlled by someone else.* You don't trust yourself.
11. *You tend to tolerate too much; you're "too nice," even to a fault.* (Someone once said that to me.) Being a "doormat" is another way to describe this. Is that true for you?
12. *You're likely underdeveloped in your education and haven't found your own voice.*
13. *You're expected to believe whatever you're told* when dealing with the person who is the primary reason for your being in Survival Mode.

The more of these characteristics you have, the more likely it is you have shut down and are in Survival Mode.

Shifting Out of Survival Mode
The **first step** is recognizing a problem exists. That is important. Without that recognition, nothing happens. When someone is only 15 percent of the person he or she always could have been, it means only 15 percent of one's true self is present. It also means he/she had to shut down by 85 percent to survive the circumstances. But doing so leaves a person vulnerable to another's control and being taken advantage of—until the reaction ends. How? By *eliminating* the reaction. This allows his/her own energy to fill in and expand. Eventually, it reduces the vulnerability and likelihood of being taken advantage of by others.

The **second step** is to decide to dismantle the Survival Mode in whatever form it takes.

The **third step** is to just start. Remember, you are the only one who knows what your Survival Mode looks like on the inside. You built it shutting down what needed to be shut down and allowing other aspects of yourself to grow a certain way without interfering with your internal plan to survive the circumstances you're in. Providing yourself with food, shelter, clothing always comes first.

If there is *any* aspect of Survival Mode going on for you, it means *you are not all here.* That's not acceptable. You need to be *all here* for your family and the world. Most of all, you need to be present for YOU—all of you.

Emotional abuse is difficult to see. There are rarely physical marks. It's usually accomplished with words and actions—or the absence of them. Immense silence is abusive, too. And in many cases, you are the only one who knows what abuse has happened—making it even harder to detect, realize, and report. Abuse of *any* kind is emotional abuse.

Emotional abuse can be as simple as a case of malfeasance (doing what should be done but doing it improperly) or nonfeasance (not doing any of what should be done). It can take years for you to figure out what happened. Yet know this: None of it was your fault.

In my case, emotional abuse caused allergy, dissociation, and fragmentation in an attempt to ease the pain. For me, Survival Mode fell apart over time and through much effort. I was able to give myself permission to shift. Journaling and meditation greatly helped me achieve that.

Percentages

Through my journaling, I sensed I had "fragmented" while growing up to be no more than 15 percent of the person I could have been. When I married, that percentage changed but to only around 20 percent. Going to law school at age 40, that percentage increased to 40. Years later—after my efforts described in Books 1 and 2—it had grown to 98 percent. That's an estimate. But after having experienced the three stories that follow, I can say I've reached 100 percent. And I feel infinitely better than that girl who grew up in the log cabin.

Looking back, the story about Missing Energy Pieces (in Book 1—*Abuse & Energy*) marked the beginning of my fragmentation reversing itself naturally. The "Hundreds of Yellow School Buses Story," the "Crash Helmet Kids Story," and the "Fifty Pairs of Legs Story" (in Book 2—*Deep Energy*) revealed more fragmentation. They also showed my fragmentation naturally reversing.

Then in January 2020, unprocessed grief came up. Three months earlier, I had returned from a four-week trip to Italy and Norway that triggered a major release. That's when I began to feel like I was coming out of shock. I cleaned closets and drawers in my condo, then went through storage units, and also had weekly 90-minute massages for more release. By November, I found myself saying out of the blue and repeating it often, "I wish Dad hadn't died. I wish Dad hadn't died."

That January, I sat down to find out why an old high school memory came up. This is what I wrote.

The High School Bus Story (Finding the Log Cabin Girl)

May 1965 Wisconsin. I heard it coming—my high school bus. It had a distinctive sound when the driver stepped on the gas pedal.

But on this day, I heard it slow down in front of the log cabin. I was standing inside in front of the living room window. I could see the bus, but I stood back far enough that the driver couldn't see me. The bus went slowly, ever so slowly, in front of my house without coming to an actual stop. I had decided to drive to school that day because Mom was away, which meant I could drive her car. But I had neglected to tell anyone about this change. The regular driver, Ruby, was looking, looking, looking for me. But I did not appear.

So, the bus went on without me... like my life going on without me. Too much was going on in this household for me to get on the bus, so I stayed behind. The bus was leaving, and I had to let it go on... without me. I'd chosen a solo path.

A part of me watched as my teenage self saw the bus come, go by slowly, then leave me behind. I then saw myself standing in my bedroom. I was 16 at the time, and Dad had not died. That event was coming in about a month.

Then I saw myself standing on the balcony looking down at the living room. Everything appeared just as it did when he died. I saw my teenage self say out loud, "They're gone. They are all gone. Finally." She said it with relief. Later, I saw her back in her bedroom playing with the wooden latch on the door. We had no locks on the interior doors, only latches.

Next, I saw that the living room door was open. She walked outside through the door to see the sunny day and green grass. She could finally breathe. Then I saw her walk back inside, leaving the door open. Next, I saw her outside wearing the kind of North Face backpack I own today. She was headed toward the awaiting bus. It was empty except for the driver. She climbed in, took a window seat and silently said "goodbye" to the now-empty house.

The driver pressed the accelerator, and the bus slowly moved on. This time I was on board. I soon found out it was headed to Dad's office.

Another part of me had stayed behind, too, at my dad's office in the City of Lake Geneva.

Closing the Coffin Lid Story
(Finding the Office Girl)

Dad represented safety for me. When he was home, I had no problem with Mom. When he died, I lost my safe haven. I could see her, a second teenage self, as she stood in Dad's office.

I saw her standing in the living room. Just standing there as if waiting for Dad to return from an appointment. She looked stunned. I could tell she knew he had died, but it had not sunk in yet. I saw her look around. Everything was just as it had been the day he died. Papers were stacked on his desk. There were two telephones. The Curtis Mathes TV/stereo console was at one end of the living room. I recalled us watching TV on Saturday nights after I made the two of us dinner. That would happen on a long day of us working with customers and showing rental houses.

Mom did not come to the office.

As I watched my teenage self, I finally said to her, "He's not coming back. He died." Her demeanor remained unchanged. She just stood there and sometimes ran her hand over the papers on the desk. I saw her stare at the lake through the large picture windows. No words were spoken.

Finally, I saw her go out the front door to the walkway leading to the street. She walked about halfway and then returned to the living room. As I stood outside the office to watch what was occurring, I saw the same high school bus arrive. The teenage girl from the log cabin was on board. The bus waited.

Then I saw this teenage girl from Dad's office standing

outside the front door with a key. She was locking the door for the final time. I watched her raise her hands to close the door, the left hand higher than the right against the door. Using both hands, she pressed the door closed—as if it were the lid of a coffin.

She slowly walked to the waiting high school bus. When she got about halfway there, a young girl (me) about five years old came barreling out of the office through the wall to catch up to the teenager walking to the bus. She was apparently a fragmented piece I had not detected when other fragmented pieces were returning. *She was NOT going to be left behind!*

The office teenage girl and the five year old climbed into the bus. They took the seat next to the log cabin teenage girl. The little girl sat on the log cabin girl's lap. The bus began to move.

I wasn't sure where this bus was going, but it didn't take long for me to sense what was occurring. It was leaving Lake Geneva and headed to my present-day condo (and me) in the Milwaukee area, about 45 minutes away. Sure enough, I could feel that they were getting closer and closer.

Finally, they arrived at my condo. I knew they were coming to merge with the rest of me that had already integrated.

Then a few weeks later in March, this reversal event occurred.

The Lumberyard Kids Story

For the Lumberyard Kids, the log cabin—with no real place to hide in—was not a safe place. That's why they left the house. But there was Dad's lumberyard in the rear of the yard and they hid there—until March 2020.

On a Thursday that March, I was working at my computer as usual. As four o'clock approached, I felt a strong sense to shut off the computer, turn out the lights, and go to my bedroom to get quiet. Solitude was needed. I rested. Then I ate dinner, went to bed early, slept well. I got up the next morning still feeling weird. I did little work and, instead, tidied up around my place. *Will I feel weird like this all day?* I wondered. A strong sense of "no" came, but I heard, *It will last most of the day.* That proved true.

After three o'clock, I began a sequence of knowing. In my mind, I was standing in the backyard of the log cabin. The swing set and sandbox were present in the same place they had been a long time ago. I used to swing on the swing set. I used to build subdivisions in the sandbox using sticks as terrace trees along the roads. With the house behind me, I faced the lumberyard, which had a series of sheds where my Dad stored supplies for building houses.

To me, the backyard was safe. So was the lumberyard. But not the house. Mom was there. It was her domain. Not mine.

The 10-year-old me sat on a rock near where I was standing, her head in her hands sobbing. She'd just heard that Dad had died. I watched her for a full 35 minutes until I saw her begin to collect herself. She was clearly aware of my being there. That's when she said, "You know, there are more of us."

I looked at her in amazement. Then I looked up past her to see the lumberyard in its entirety. Until that point, I had focused only on her. Now, I could see hundreds of us. Our ages varied from very young to age 10 or so. They had the kind of long hair I had back then. They knew who I was. And they were happy to see me.

I knew what it felt like to have just a few of them merge. With hundreds, that could be a problem. Yet I knew they needed to integrate and questioned how long that might take.

I was impressed by this 10 year old who greeted me sitting on that rock. As the oldest of the group, she had become the appointed leader of these fragmented parts. She stood watch for anyone who might come by—and specifically if *I* came back for them.

I didn't know they were even there. But something significant was happening for me to stop work that day and rest. What started on a Thursday took about 23 hours for them to merge into my psyche, although I knew it would take weeks and weeks for them all to be completely integrated into my energy field.

The 10-year-old me had kept them all together. She'd also kept them informed.

By 10 o'clock on Saturday morning, I had my answer to the question "How long will it take?" I always knew they would re-enter the energy field from which they came. I wondered if I could withstand the process of integrating so many at a time when I was focused on my writing. Then I received an "okay" from deep inside.

If you have you ever sensed fragments within you, how would you describe them?

The Lumberyard Kids knew how to integrate. It is like being in an elevator presumably filled to capacity, and then the doors open to a crowd of people wanting to get in. At first, you gasp because you think, "There's no way they'll all fit. The elevator walls are finite. They do not stretch (or so we think)!"

Still, the crowd enters the elevator. There's jockeying around and even elbowing, but somehow, they all fit in. Amazing!

"It's Over—Finally!"
A few months before this happened, I heard the phrase "it's over" numerous times, but I didn't know what it meant. Then after the Log Cabin Girl and the Office Girl fragments returned followed by the Lumberyard Kids, I heard these words: "My childhood is over. Finally!"

Inside, I sensed it was indeed finally over. I felt a difference.

In a meditation, I asked, "So, what happened to me?" In a day or so, an old memory popped into my head. *Why this memory? And why now?* I didn't know. I just sat down and paid attention. In fact, I relived it.

The Linn Pier Close Call Story

One hot September day after school, a group of us went down to the lake for one last swim. Because it was after Labor Day, no lifeguards were on duty to enforce the usual rules. We could do whatever we wanted—like running on the pier, jumping in areas off limits to swimmers, swimming under the pier, standing on the posts to jump in from a higher position. Fun!

I rode my bicycle to Linn Pier, dropped it on the grass, and began running onto the pier. I was 13. Dad's death was about three years away, so I wasn't carrying that burden. But I knew this memory of an event would help me understand something I needed to know.

I ran the length of the pier and jumped into the lake at a deep part—so deep, I couldn't get a push off the floor of the lake after jumping in.

I went straight down. As I slowly came up to the surface, one of the other kids jumped in behind me—in the same spot. About my age, he was taller and bigger than me. He dropped into the water right on top of me as I was coming up. It knocked the air out of my lungs and pushed me down deeper than I'd been. I didn't reach the bottom either time. And like before, I couldn't get a push off from the bottom to get to the surface faster. Instead, I had to swim vertically with every stroke being hard work.

I was out of air, and my lungs burned.

This memory represented two events that had pushed me deep emotionally. One pushdown was by Mom. Then, as I was coming up from that, getting my driver's license, and anticipating being in the clear by attending college, another event occurred. Dad's passing.

It pushed me down deeper than ever.

This memory kept coming back to me as an answer to my meditation question. More than that, it gave me a visual, an understanding, of what happened—truthfully, what my heart already knew.

All of these stories show *why* it's important to dismantle your Survival Mode and *how* it naturally happened for me. Knowing what occurred is one thing; successfully *restoring* yourself energetically is another.

8

Trust Your Natural Instincts

*Sometimes trusting your natural instincts
is all you have.*

Even though I grew up white, I was the Anti-Majoritarian Difficulty within my own family. The "problem" was I was female; therefore, the message I received was "I was not to be included." Trusting my natural instincts helped me overcome the emotional abuse I felt in my childhood. That trust sent me to law school in 1988 as a first step in creating a better life for myself. Here's how I came to understand why that had been the first step for me.

During my first year in law school, I was required to take

a course in Real Property law. We had a visiting professor who assigned a lot of reading outside the normal textbook. It would prove prophetic.

One of the professor's assignments described the experience of Native Americans when the "white man" invaded their territory. In the readings, the white invaders labeled Native Americans the "Anti-Majoritarian Difficulty." They bore this label because they did not assimilate into the white man's dominant governing culture in what eventually became the United States. Instead, thousands of Native Americans were massacred and thousands more moved from their homelands onto reservations in various parts of the country.

This kind of treatment describes what can happen when we don't submit to the controlling powers—on a large scale, yes, but even in one's home.

Treasure Trove—My True Self

Another reading on Real Property law required us to understand laws about discovering a treasure trove. In Book 1 in this series, you might recall how, by going deep inside, I found a treasure trove—my true self. I discovered parts of me I didn't know had been missing until they came back. Restored. The law about discovering a treasure trove makes it clear that the treasure belonged to the finder. That would be me—the person who found the treasured missing parts.

I took the time to do this extra reading and a question about it appeared on our first-semester final exam. Because I knew the material, I nailed the answer. I wasted no words, making it concise, tightly written, and to the point. Later, I found out mine was one of the top three answers in the class. I learned that when the professor invited our class to his office to show how a law school exam question *should* be answered.

Imagine me sitting in the professor's office looking to review his selected best answers, reading each one closely, and then pulling up the next example—mine!

During my first semester of law school, I had worried about making it through, given that 100 percent of our grade was based on this final exam. *A bit like life,* I thought. But getting recognized for that exam question told me, *Yes, I do belong in law school.* It was a message contrary to the unspoken messages I'd heard all my life from within my own family.

Only in recent years did I recognize why the phrase "Anti-Majoritarian Difficulty" struck me. It was an early "pinging" that led me to understand how the concept described *me and my role in our family.* Apparently, I had something worthwhile to write. And I needed to go to law school to write it.

The Anti-Majoritarian Difficulty

Even though the plight of Native Americans (both then and now) differs significantly from my personal situation, similarities can be drawn. Historically, just as Native Americans didn't assimilate with the majority culture, I did not assimilate within my own family. They fought against white control over them. I resisted, too. In fact, I was criticized and disciplined by my mother for *not* submitting to her controlling, abusive power.

Being the Anti-Majoritarian Difficulty—either within one's own family or within one's own country—requires going into Survival Mode and subsequently settling for being a percentage of who one could have been. Our nation's history and present-day dominant society continues to support a form of Anti-Majoritarian Difficulty by excluding minorities such as Blacks, Hispanics, Asians, Native Americans, LGBTQ people, and more. Many turn to Survival Mode to keep going.

For me, I sensed the process of Survival Mode was well underway before I turned six years old. It took decades before I could come out of Survival Mode, primarily because I didn't know it even existed. And by not knowing what I know now, all I had was trusting my natural instincts to eventually get out of that way of existing.

Following my natural instincts was my path ahead—and it could be yours, too. As an advantage, you will know more starting out than I ever did by hearing about my experiences and adding your own instincts. These can pave the way for you to *become the person you always could have been.*

> *Following my natural instincts was my path ahead—and it could be yours, too.*

9

Listen to Your Intuition

The three most important tools of energy you'll ever have are trusting your natural instincts, listening to your intuition, and learning to set intentions. They can serve as your Flashlight in times of darkness.

BEFORE WE SET OUT ON WHAT COULD BE A LONG journey, we normally look for information from people who have gone before us. *What's their best advice? What do they recommend we do first?* Asking is a natural thing to do.

But there are more answers you'll need for this kind of a trip—answers that only *you* know. And those answers can be found only deep inside. These are the kind that require you to listen, *really listen*, to your intuition, possibly in ways you've never done before.

Perhaps no one has ever taught you how to listen to your intuition or given you permission to do so. I will do that on these pages the best I can by sharing my experiences and holding your hand going forward.

Analytical thinking is a strength of mine and may be one of yours, too. But I've learned it can get in the way of *becoming who you always could have been.* Analysis can be problematic when you want to *honestly* listen to yourself. Why? Because people can rely on heavy analytical thinking as a coping mechanism. It certainly was a coping mechanism for me.

> *Analysis can be problematic when you want to honestly listen to yourself. Why? Because people can rely on heavy analytical thinking as a coping mechanism. I certainly did.*

Even as a teenager, I'd lie on the sofa for hours just thinking, which tells me my Survival Mode kicked in early on in my life. That also tells me analytical thinking will fight me in making any changes—that is, until my analytical thinking shifts to see things differently.

But let me share a technique that has helped me to put analytical thinking in its place. I call this practice "Tell Your Analytical Mind to Get in the Back Seat So the Rest of You Can Drive." Try it for yourself!

Tell Your Analytical Mind to Get in the Back Seat So the Rest of You Can Drive Story

"What are you doing that for? You should go this way. We always go this way. It's the shortest way. What are you doing? *Nobody does it this way!*"

Often, things would be going along fine until I could hear my analytical mind shouting phrases like these. So, early on, to tap into my intuition, I instructed my analytical mind to "get in the back seat of the car and just watch me drive."

Mostly, this command worked. But there were times I sensed my analytical mind figuring out things to the point it was *sure* it knew what was coming next. Then I could hear these words from the back seat: "Oh, I get it; we're going to do this!" Like any experienced driver would do, I instructed my analytical mind to "back off." I then continued to do what was planned all along.

There were even times when my analytical mind wanted to grab the wheel and steer in the direction it thought I should go. "No!" I said, instructing it to "get back in your seat and be quiet." Once, when it even got close enough to the driver's seat (in my imagination of course), I had to "slap" its hand and tell it to return to the back seat. This worked. It always did.

Over time, finally (and I mean *finally*) my analytical mind saw the wisdom of what my intuition was doing—steering me out of the kind of internal trouble that had been years in the making. I realized my analytical mind was clueless about how much trouble I was in and how I was stuck in Survival Mode. But slowly, my mind came to understand how efficiently my intuition could raise up and deal with all my issues—*before it was too late.*

Have there been moments when you wanted to listen to your intuition but didn't? What happened?

Your intuition works by coordinating all your innate abilities and subtle energy sensors, which are directly connected to the all-encompassing God and universal energy.

As your intuitive part that's been shut down to facilitate your Survival Mode begins to operate normally, you'll likely notice you do things differently. This is what the internal command of RESTORE is all about. You may hear that word when you listen intently to your intuition. Honor it. Nurture it. Listening to your intuition is a skill. It is educating your mind.

If you are in Survival Mode, now is the time to end it. Make it your goal to nurture yourself to become *100 percent of the person you could always have been.* Why? Because all of you is needed. You are needed here for yourself and for others in your life.

Key Points

Here in your reading of *Peace & Energy*, I want to remind you of these key points:

- You *are* more than you *think* you are.
- You *know* more than you *think* you do.
- You are educating your mind.
- You are asking, "What do I need to know?"
- Energy was the problem; energy is *your* solution.

- No one has ever walked in *your* shoes nor have you likely walked in *theirs*.

To you, my reader, it is time to shine your strongest Flashlight on these key points for yourself. How? By trusting your natural instincts, listening to your intuition, and—as described in the next chapter—learning to set your intentions.

Listening to and honoring my intuition—even without knowing the "why" of what it wanted me to do—has been among the smartest things I've ever done.

10

The Value of Setting Intentions

Heed the old saying "Be careful what you wish for."

WHEN YOU LEARN JUST HOW MUCH SETTING intentions affects your ability to create, you will also learn this allows you the opportunity to specifically direct your intuition.

With intentions, you are communicating what you desire. Yes, your intuition will feel at first like having your own personal genie. However, at some point, the responsibility of what you are *actually* creating begins to set in. That's why you must understand how intentions work. And just as trusting and listening turn on your Flashlight, so does setting intentions. This action tells your deep self where to point the Flashlight—that is, it spells out what you aim to create for yourself.

And that's why I agree with the saying "Be careful what you wish for."

Picks Up on the Vibration

Years ago, I did not know what an intention was. But I was fairly certain it had something to do with stating what I wanted—in other words, my intent. Universal energy picks up the vibration of what you desire, and that vibration could be amazingly wonderful or absolutely hellish. It isn't judged; it's simply received.

In my view, intentions (whether they are thought, said, or written) should be set in the positive. This world does not need more negative vibrations!

Can you *accidentally* set an intention? Yes, I believe that is possible.

"What Needs to be Said" Story

When I was writing Book 1 of this series, someone asked how I got this way—all the visions, epiphanies, sensing, hearings, knowings, and intuitive nudgings. I honestly didn't have an answer, so I began to look back in time for one. The best I could surmise is that at age 12 or 13—after the epiphany about something being wrong in the house—I must have felt my life was "toast." At that time, I had already formed a close, strong connection with God, so I made up a prayer that I repeated a lot. It went like this: *Dear God, If something needs to be said, help me to say it. If something needs to be done, help me to do it. If something needs **not** to be said, help me to **not** say it. If something needs to be **not** done, help me to **not** do it.*

Looking back, I think that prayer put me on the life path I've been on. Knowing what I know today, writing as I am now and backing it up with speaking, this fulfills the "say what needs to be said" part. And for the "if something needs to be done" part, I fulfill that with publishing books.

I believe that this prayer, composed so long ago, in effect acted like an intention. It tapped into universal energy and generated all the other factors that come together to make something happen. These factors during this experience would include all the stories, visions, unraveling, and living of the story itself, so I could say what needs to be said.

The phrase "what needs to be *said*" also implies "what needs to be *heard*" by others. That's why I write and speak about what might be their emotional and energetic pain as well as my own—and why the title is *Peace & Energy*. My premise is that *peace begins on the inside and nowhere else*. After writing that statement in the first book, it only took me three books to find out the meaning of those words for myself and for you, and why those words were the right ones. When there is no peace on the inside, there cannot be peace on the outside. A reaction that occurred sometime in your life can cause a shutdown of who you always could have been. Until that is corrected by receiving the energy nurturing you should have received, it will continue. Peace on the inside will elude you. Remember, what happened to you probably happened to the people you reacted to. That doesn't excuse them, but it can make it harder to be angry or hate them or even hate yourself.

Do intentions matter? Absolutely they do. And here are more examples of why.

Powerful Examples of Intention

In 2015, one of the persons running for president stated he would say or do "whatever it takes" to win the 2016 U.S. presidential race. That was an example of stating a strong intention. He said he intended to gain peoples' votes, so he would come out on top no matter the means. An intention can be said powerfully—so powerfully that people comply without realizing they are.

I suspect my mother set a powerful intention, too. It would have been something that reflected her fear about not getting enough—a fear I became aware of after John's passing. When felt strongly, those words can be enough to communicate an intention and affect one's ability to make a wish come true.

For my brother John, his probable intention was someday seeing fulfilled his mother's verbal promise of inheriting the entire estate. In fact, by being the first-born male in our family, he believed he was *entitled* to the full inheritance, despite what Dad's 1965 will said. But John's only sibling (me) challenged Mom's will that intended to fulfill that promise. As you know from reading this book, he didn't get what he wished for. He was overruled by someone who was stronger—his only sibling and her wish to be treated fairly.

Be careful that someone hasn't set intentions for you that will not benefit you. They could be, in fact, to your detriment.

Be careful that someone hasn't set intentions for you that will not benefit you. They could be, in fact, to your detriment.

Families might have intentions that run within the family for generations. They can be unspoken, but you become aware of them by the behavior you see. They expect you to shut down and adopt those intentions—or else. Yet if their intentions go against your true nature, watch out. Survival Mode can be triggered.

As stated in this book, I had been locked in Survival Mode for decades. This story provides a sense of how I used the power of intention to begin transforming my life, starting in 1997.

"I Don't Have a Life" Story

July 1997. I had been divorced for over a year when I slowly began to realize I didn't have much of a life. So, I decided to do something about it.

Sitting in my apartment, I started a list. At this point, Mom would be still alive for another eight years. Journaling, meditation, and counseling would begin in a few months.

Writing would begin in two years. But I didn't know any of this yet. I wondered, *What does it mean to "have a life"?*

With only a candle next to me, I began to write down exactly what I thought having a life meant. Career, housing, friends, good health, good relationships, and even some tennis from time to time. That's what I wrote on the paper I had on my lap. My list was actually longer than this, but I did put tennis on it, even though it was last. I hadn't played in a long time. And I loved it! But I remember including it was almost like a whim, and I didn't expect anything to come of it.

Nothing happened right away. But within two weeks, I felt nudgings to act. Out of all the things on that list, tennis was the first stirring to come. I felt the need to find a tennis club where I could play all year round. I didn't blow the feeling off. Instead, I acted on it—honoring it. I did so without knowing how important this was going to be. I checked out two places and one was perfect. It even hosted a social mixer every Friday night where tennis players would show up with food to share and play some tennis.

My intuition was right. It was through this club I met two wonderful women—one at the tennis mixer and the other at another club social event, a baseball game. Looking back, it's absolutely clear they were meant to be part of my new emerging life. And that having their friendship would turn out to be just as foundational as any job or career decision.

At the baseball game, I met Margery. I didn't know anyone at this event, but the club planner knew her, and she seated us together. Margery was there with her son, an expert on baseball. She was an expert on etiquette and had also traveled the world.

Since that fortuitous meeting, Margery has taught me a great deal both formally in her classes and informally on travel and manners.

The other woman, Rebecca, was a financial planner. We met at Big Bob's Tennis Mixer one Friday night. She was there with her husband. We hit it off. Mind you, I had little equity back then, but that has since changed. She has stayed right with me for every step, both as a planner and a friend. Rebecca assisted me greatly with the financial challenges I faced during the fight for my inheritance and through the handling of two estates.

Looking back even further in time to law school, I met another wonderful woman, Marilyn, who also supported me in my inheritance fight. Later, she helped to get me to the level of legal expertise I would need. I can still remember standing in the library during my last year on the first day of Litigation class. The professor told us we needed to partner with someone. I then realized everyone was standing next to someone. They already knew they needed a partner. I didn't. But as luck would have it, Marilyn was standing a short distance from me without a partner. She quickly asked me to partner with her. I, of course, said yes. It was a good match.

My new life continues to unfold, stemming back to 1997, with new people entering it and enriching my journey. Today, all three of these magnificent women remain in my life, still educating and supporting me. Over the years, I have met even more men and women who have come to my aid—many who, when our paths crossed, became longtime friends. All showing me the things I never knew. I thank them all.

You never know who will come your way to take this ride of life with you. That's why I stress the importance of paying attention to *everything* going on around you. Once you seriously turn on your Flashlight, help will come. You might not recognize or realize it as help when it first arrives but know that it *will* come.

What Really Needs to Be Said?

Looking back, there's an outstanding question: *What really needs to be said?* I believe the answer is this: The human condition we are experiencing today is a direct result of us not recognizing the Human Energy System that exists in each of us. This lack of recognition needs to be corrected.

Exposing the authoritarians, the emotional abuse they do, and the tragic results they can create is vital to our understanding of life and will lead to changes for the better. The authoritarian does not respect laws—be it the laws of the nation or anyone's personal laws (boundaries).

That's because our laws, in particular federal laws, were written to protect our rights as individuals. The Bill of Rights and our Constitution say it best: *We the People . . .* Beyond that, personal laws are boundaries we set for ourselves and others who want to interact with us.

Survival Mode is best dealt with by nurturing the percentage of one's true self that is actually present—no matter how low that percentage may be and no matter what circumstances caused it to be that way. Remember, I was only 10 to 15 percent of my true self for a long time. That gradually changed as I began to take the nurturing steps that naturally made the difference.

Trusting, Listening, and Setting Intentions are some of the key nurturing steps you need to be the person you always could have been.

Foundational Energy Elements

Know this, too. There are many foundational energy elements needed to sustain human life on this planet. Without these foundational elements, we do not thrive, and we do not grow as much as we could. But unlike gardens that need only sunlight, water, clean air, and good soil to grow, we need more. These foundational elements are needed for humans to thrive and grow.

The 12 chapters that follow provide information on how you can dismantle Survival Mode for yourself and restore your own Human Energy System, regardless of whatever condition it's in. This experience-based knowledge will help you increase your own energy percentage points and eliminate what doesn't belong. What doesn't belong for sure? Any vulnerability to being controlled by others.

Although these 12 chapters appear in a particular order, you can follow them in a sequence that intuitively suits you. The best place to start is noticing what grabs your attention, but I encourage you to still go through them all. Even if some topics may not seem to apply, they will likely assist you in other ways. Pay attention, and you'll see!

Specifically, watch for patterns as they will repeat themselves. Seeing a pattern can ease the strain of not knowing what is coming next. Also, realize you don't have to know why (or how) something should be a certain way. The analytical reason for it emerges eventually, but here's a warning: waiting until you understand *why* can cost you valuable time.

Beginning with Chapter Eleven, you will read about actions you can take (immediately) to begin releasing Survival Mode and its long-term effects. Once upon a time, Survival Mode saved your life. Now, it may be holding you in a place you no longer need to be. It's time to be YOU—because All of You is needed for the difficult task of rebuilding our lives and our nation.

Don't wait to use your Flashlight (Trust your Natural Instincts, Listen to your Intuition, and Learn to Set Intentions). Begin to use it now! Working with the Human Energy System can restore you to be the person you always could have been. It becomes your Flashlight for when times are uncertain and dark. Regard it as your personal beacon of hope.

11

ℒearn to "See" and "Hear" Properly

*Seeing and hearing properly means to
see and hear both worlds—the physical one
we know and the other one—energy.*

LEARNING TO "SEE" AND "HEAR" PROPERLY MEANS THAT we interact with both the physical and energy worlds every day—if we realize it or not. And we need to learn to do it properly, fully.

During your everyday routine, it can be difficult to open up to both worlds, especially if fragments are involved. For that reason, it is possible you might be receiving information throughout the day, but if you aren't paying attention, what you've asked for will be (as the old saying goes) "falling on deaf ears." When that happens repeatedly, the information will simply stop coming because no one is listening. You *want* to listen. And as poets have been telling us for years, "the eyes are the window to the soul." You *want* to see, too.

This story gives you an idea of what "seeing" and "hearing" can be.

Which Coffee Cup in the Morning Story

I look forward to a cup of coffee in the morning. It nurtures my soul for the day. Perhaps it does that for you, too. First, with my black slippers on my feet and usually still wearing my comfortable pajamas, I make my way toward the windows and plants in my living room. Raising the blinds, I hear the sound they make. It's a mundane kind of a sound, grounding and nurturing, that serves to start my day right.

Watching the blinds go up, my eyes (my pupils) are noticing the weather outside. Snowy, rainy, cloudy, sunny? Whatever the weather, it feels grounding, too. "Earth. I am here. Another day has begun. Now to the kitchen..."

Walking into the kitchen, I ask, "Which cup is needed today?" I have learned to let my eyes make that selection. "Which cupboard door do I open first? Then which cup?" My eyes *show* me. The process goes something like this: My gaze first goes to which of the two cupboard doors to open. Okay. It's the one on the left today. Then I slowly let my eyes scan the cups. Today, it's a black one I purchased from Starbucks on a road trip in 2019. There is no analytical reason for picking this one, except it was black, which reminds me of the universe and its infinite qualities. I never hear any words expressed from inside telling me why I make this selection. It's simply *this one "feels" right*.

Often, the cup I choose gives me a heads-up to an event soon to occur that I need to pay attention to. On this day, I sense the black cup will help me with my writing and creative thinking. I will spare you all the details of which coffee or tea, whether it's with milk or cream or not; my answers vary all the time. But one kind has remained a favorite over the recent years: a refrigerated cold brew coffee from California. I used to live there. Luckily, my local grocer here carries the same coffee. When I write, that's generally the coffee I choose. Living in Wisconsin when it's cold outside, I heat it. *How I miss that California experience.*

But there is one thing more about it: the shape of the bottle itself. It has a gentle curve to it—a familiar curve. I draw it when I journal and often when I write as well. That gentle curve appears in my furnishings, too. It was there long before I found that particular coffee. Reaching for it in the refrigerator first thing in the morning before I sit down to journal or write speaks volumes. It's a reminder: *This is me.*

My morning ritual is one of those emotional moments that help me start my day. Something that might seem mundane can both ground and nurture you if you are willing to notice.

Grieving is another example of how to "see" and "hear" properly, because when grief is unfolding, it can be especially hard to "see" and "hear" anything. Yet, much can be learned when you allow grief to become a descriptive lesson.

First, learn to recognize grieving when it comes. Survival Mode can block any deeply rooted emotional response to loss you've experienced, preventing it from being processed. Why? Because you have blocked it so you don't *feel it*. And being able to *fully feel* is counter to life in Survival Mode.

Such a moment came to me recently.

A Conversation with "Dad"— a Grief Unfolding Story

"Tranquil Sunset" it was called. I wasn't enamored by this picture puzzle, but when I ordered it online, this selection seemed right. As I was compiling a list of energy needs for this book, I knew a different picture puzzle needed to be worked on before starting Tranquil Sunset. There always seems to be a specific order, so I honored it.

After opening the cupboard in my utility room, my eyes scanned the puzzles waiting to be put together. "Cozy Retreat"—a Ravensburger puzzle. My eyeballs locked on to it. "Okay," I thought. "That's the one for today." And Cozy Retreat took its place at the end of my dining room table until it was time. That came a few days later.

As I put together all the pieces of Cozy Retreat, I felt a sense of calm. This puzzle pictured a cottage with a woman holding her cup of coffee/tea, a cat curled up next to her, a dog on the floor snuggled on a rug. It had candles, books, a laptop, an alarm clock among other items. A cozy retreat, producing a picture of calmness and solitude.

I began Cozy Retreat on a Tuesday and finished it within 24 hours. Record time! But it would take another week for the next puzzle to come forward to help me release the grief that the Office Girl (from Chapter Seven) had pent up inside.

Tranquil Sunset featured a sunset and mountains—tranquil indeed.

Also 500 pieces like Cozy Retreat. I began working it on Wednesday. And I finished it the same Wednesday. What would this puzzle do for me? Lots.

Outside, I heard the sound of a buzzsaw. Someone was trimming trees nearby for much of the afternoon as I worked this puzzle. In the past, I would have noticed the sound, possibly even be irritated by it, but I never would have noticed that the sound had meaning. On this day, it did. I've come to appreciate how following my nudges can be exactly what *I* need to do.

Here are some of the lead-up events to the day I finished Tranquil Sunset:

Monday, I had a hair color treatment with a new stylist doing a sleeked-down version of my hair. She asked what I wanted; I just left it up to her. That proved to be a trigger, reminding me of the sleek, long, straight hairstyle of Barbra Streisand. It also reminded me of when I was 16. When no one else was home, I would sing along with Barbra's music, not holding anything back!

Tuesday that week, I didn't write a lot. Instead, I moved a second lamp into my office to improve the lighting. That in turn caused me to arrange my desk differently. With darkness coming in late afternoon in Wisconsin (it was October), this change would be good, I thought. Other things got rearranged, too.

Wednesday, I wrote most of the morning and emailed with my editor. And I ate. (I always eat when I write. Go figure.) I had cause to review photos in Books 1 and 2. One of Dad in Book 2, *Deep Energy*, stood out.

I had opened the new puzzle that morning, scissoring open the plastic bag and pulling out some of the border pieces. As the morning progressed, I put a few pieces together whenever I needed a break. Then things really started happening!

As 2 p.m. approached, I felt the need to stop what I was doing at the computer. Without a word, I got up and turned out the office lights, leaving the computer and printer still on. It seemed important to relax and take an hour-long break. After getting "off the page," I let my mind go wherever it wanted to go. Then a new text "dinged" on my phone. A friend in California sent me a photo of a diamond wristwatch her father had given her years before when she graduated from nursing school. I already knew she wanted me to have this watch when she passes. It's a Bulova. Coincidentally, Dad had given me a Bulova wristwatch when I graduated from eighth grade (no diamonds, though). Seeing the Bulova photo just after I studied the photo of Dad (page 66 in Book 2) didn't strike me as important. But it apparently was.

A little after 3 p.m., without a word, I walked to the sunset/

mountain picture puzzle at the end of the dining room table and began to work it. My eyes were glued to a spot across the room. Over the years, I've learned that means I am sensing someone is there, so I began to talk and talk and talk. I spoke out loud. For hours. I knew I was talking to Dad and telling him EVERYTHING that had happened—from when Mom wrote in her diary (described in Chapter Four) to the present. I talked to him *as if he were standing right there.* I needed that. But more precisely, I knew it was the *16-year-old Office Girl* who was unloading everything she needed to say about Mom and John, about Dad's leaving, about her whole life.

Like putting together puzzle pieces, the pieces of that Office Girl had integrated into me seven months before this writing. All the while, I worked the puzzle in record time, completing it by 9:30 p.m. that night. My hands were constantly picking up pieces, and when my eyes weren't fixed on the spot across the room, they looked for where to place those pieces.

All this time, except for a few quiet moments around 7 p.m., my speaking to Dad never stopped.

I call what happened "grieving unfolding." Doing the puzzle served to break up the internal blockage—the grief—with vibration. (Think of health professionals in hospitals who use sonar to break up kidney stones—same thing, but it is a picture puzzle breaking up grief.) I needed to say the words and hear the sound of the buzzsaw outside telling me I am "buzz sawing" my way through something.

The puzzle became my portal to wherever Dad was. I could "see" his face enough to see his lips were moving when he asked

The puzzle became my portal to wherever Dad was. I could "see" his face enough to see his lips were moving when he asked me questions. me questions. Yet, there was no sound, which is characteristic of the dimensional difference between us. I could sense the words he was saying via vibration while assuming he could "hear" or "sense" my words—all of them.

After I finished the puzzle that evening, I stayed up a few hours sitting in silence. About midnight, I went to sleep. During the night, I felt a presence in my bedroom that was not right. I heard a cough that wasn't mine. I ordered that presence OUT of my room and pointed to the window. "GET OUT!" It did. Not right away, but it eventually left.

I realized this was a negative energy. Dad's vibration was higher than Mom's—that is, not as suppressed as I believe hers was. Because mine has been cleaning out what doesn't belong, I sensed how my power has increased. This "thing" had to respond to *my* order—not the other way around. This could have been the "dark cloud" Mom said she had, yet she never knew what it really was.

Along with my newly arranged desk and additional lamp for more lighting, this event helped me feel more urgency and passion than ever before—to write.

Your Physical and Energy Needs

Always ask yourself: *Are you meeting both your physical needs as well as your energy needs?* The next chapter addresses energy needs more specifically, but this chapter shows you how to pick up different vibrations around you and realize their significance. Sometimes sights and sounds will catch your attention; sometimes they won't. On this journey, you can assume they *will* capture it when the issue is important enough.

It is believed that Helen Keller contracted rubella or scarlet fever as a small child, and that caused her to lose her sight and hearing. The 1962 movie *The Miracle Worker* detailed her life as a child. The movie shows a famous scene at the water pump where, for the first time, Helen realized the water she was feeling pouring over her hand had a name. This was the moment when something she could feel but could not see opened a whole new life for her. Helen Keller went on to have an extraordinary life.

As you have likely determined, the kind of "seeing" and "hearing" I'm referring to is more than what you normally experience with your two eyes and ears. Sights and sounds can have a special relevance to you, whether it's a police siren, a car horn, letters by themselves or in words, numbers, photos, pictures, shapes, drawings, objects, a cough or sneeze—almost anything. A certain sight or sound will remind you of something or someone, yet it can have a much deeper meaning. You might cough when nothing (such as swallowing wrong or having an actual cold) triggered it, yet you know that *something* did. When it happens, ask yourself this question: Is your deep internal self attempting to tell you something that has no words? No one else could have a clue what that meaning could be, but inside, YOU do. Generally, that requires noticing the actual (physical) and the vibrational (energy) at the same time. Taking this further, when I'm conversing with someone and do a "two cough" (as in cough-cough one after the other) for no apparent reason, I know it's an internal signal for me to stop. I should not go further with that line of conversation or even the subject we are discussing.

Why this happens is not clear to me, but I have learned to "hear" it and honor the message my cough-cough is sending. I recommend you do, too.

Similar to the two-cough example but yet different, my left hand often reaches up to my neck and gently caresses my throat. This happens when I'm speaking or writing about a difficult subject. It's as if I'm giving myself a hug of emotional support to fully express all the words that have not ever been said and *should be said now.*

A Deep Voice

Early in my recovery experience, I heard a deep voice come from my throat—a kind of gurgle. I could tell words were part of it, but I couldn't understand them. The voice was deeper than mine. Back then, when I'd casually ask myself a question out loud, I'd answer back—but in a low voice. After all the integration of fragments that has occurred since then and especially recently, only one voice comes out. That tells me a great deal of built-up energy was apparently stuck in my throat.

A point not yet said (but needs to be) is how our word for "heart" combines two words—*hear it.* Perhaps that's the energy of that word—meaning we should "hear it" (energy). Interesting, isn't it?

With the eyes being the window to the soul, I'd go one step further than the poets. Perhaps the word we use for the center

With the eyes being the window to the soul, I'd go one step further than the poets.

of each eye—pupil—suggests the soul is a student. Pupil is another word for student. Pay attention to your pupils, especially when they stare at a word or an object seemingly on their own. Are they telling you something you've wondered about? Are they trying to show you something? For me, this kind of connection started years ago, soon after I began to journal. The moment I realize my eyes are trying to communicate something to my brain, a simple, quiet feeling registers, and I sense *this is right*. Often, this sense is extremely subtle and can be easily missed.

Paying attention to your behaviors are highly instructive when you're taking apart Survival Mode. *What you can't see matters. It's energy.* And all things are energy.

Taking Apart Survival Mode

As a starting point, I suggest you ask yourself these questions:

"What do I need to know about myself? About the people who raised me?"

"What percentage of their complete selves were they as you were growing up?"

"What percentage of their complete selves are they now?"

"What percentage am I today?"

12

Supporting Your Energy System

*Coconut-something every day—even just
smelling it—supports my energy system.*

FOOD. SHELTER. CLOTHING. THESE ARE WHAT WE ARE customarily told will meet our physical needs. Sure. But that's only for the physical. We need more than that, because we are more than just physical. Your body is the physical housing for your soul.

Soul is energy, and that is who we are inside. We have personal energy needs inside as well. And when our inner energy needs aren't being met, we suffer.

One of the fastest ways to end Survival Mode is to support

your energy system by understanding you have energy needs, knowing what specific needs are for you, then actively addressing these needs.

The Foundational Elements of the Human Energy System
Similar to vitamins, there are elements your soul needs to receive every day to build up in your energy system and be available for when you need them. On the days when little new energy is coming in, you can draw from the stored-up amount. That will keep your circuits humming and your energy flowing.

Light is a good example of something that cannot be readily stored. For that reason, we have searched for other remedies to provide what we need. For people in Wisconsin, a common solution is to spend winters in places such as Arizona, Hawaii, and Florida—to name a few. Using special lamps that provide "natural" light is another. (I have two of these lights.) Research shows Vitamin D helps our bodies, and I suspect (to an extent) that works. But light is light and what it does for you can't be quantified in a pill or artificially. For many, though, getting more light can be a good start.

The list that follows is not the be-all-end-all. In fact, it's just the start of a longer list. Then, in the chapters that follow, I address most of the Foundational Elements of the Human Energy System.

Above all, though, Safety is the number one issue. It is not included in this list; rather, it is addressed in detail in Chapter Thirteen.

Souls need a *VARIETY* of:

- Light—direct sunlight, daylight, natural light
- Color—all colors, even black (absorbs all) and white (reflects all)
- Scent—perfume, aromas, odors
- Texture—smooth, rough, shapes (It's touch, but it is also sight.)
- Movement—exercise (all kinds), flight of birds, butterflies, dance, and so on
- Sound—music, street noise, sirens, ambulances, voices . . . any kind of sound
- Taste—both in food and in personal choices (such as taste in décor)
- Touch—feel and sight (e.g., seeing a loved one)
- Love—shared energy with another living being, including love of yourself
- Space—expansiveness
- Grounding—meditation, journaling, root vegetables, earth

Recognizing you have your own energy needs, learning what they are and how to meet them can be key to eliminating/reversing Survival Mode. Such realizations can facilitate the return and integration of any fragmented pieces you may have, bringing them back "home" where they belong. Because you've done this, you've begun nurturing your physical as well as your energy body correctly.

For me, recognition started a number of years ago in two venues: at work by noticing how much I loved the color of Post-it®

Notes and at home by enjoying the color of washcloths. In recent days, that recognition has grown into much more.

My Foundational Personal Energy Needs Story

I live in a small condo and to help me ride out the dark winter of 2020-2021, I leased an apartment nearby that was larger, brighter. This apartment gave me a safe place to write or just decompress because of the pandemic. Having another space to go to considerably expanded my world.

While at the apartment, I learned what a difference it can make when certain energy needs are being met. For example, on one Monday, I brought my lunch to this apartment where I could gaze out over the green nature conservancy just outside my windows. I intentionally walked to the balcony door and opened it, then I faced east where I could see sunrises and moonrises. Being three floors up, my sight line was right at treetop level, so I could see a lot of green and open, expansive sky—usually blue but sometimes with white cloud formations moving. I noticed the poplar trees and the sound of their rustling leaves. Also nearby was West Bluemound Road with all its normal sounds of traffic. *This setting did something for me.*

On that Monday, I noticed "it" for the first time. (Although I knew when I leased the apartment that certain aspects made the space feel right, I just couldn't identify them. That day, they were hitting me over the head!) As I ate, I paid close attention both to my food and to what I saw and experienced outside through the open sliding glass door. My eyes actively took it all in. I didn't feel any particular emotion. Joy? Happiness? Whatever it was, it was incredibly subtle. And I could not identify a single word that would describe my feeling. It took a whole day for a primary word to come to me.

FOUNDATIONAL. And secondarily, **TRANQUIL**.

Not a lot of emotion in either word, I thought. And I could barely feel what "it" was—though it was clearly *present*. And *important*.

That's when I realized *many* Foundational Energy Elements were present during that simple lunch experience. I knew that by having these elements in this place, I could recharge my batteries in a way I could not at my condo.

With these elements being satisfied and allowing me to recharge, I realized, *This is the foundation upon which I can build. It is Tranquility. It is Peace.* This is when I realized I could replace *Abuse* with *Peace* by meeting my own foundational energy needs.

I believe this elemental truth applies to each of us. It's like when you build a house or any structure, you need footings to start. This simple apartment—with no furniture except for two chairs and a few kitchen items—is where I started. It represents the kind of footings I always needed to have in place—and didn't.

Another thing you can do to tune into your Foundational Energy Elements is to apply the rules of energy flow. These rules make it clear that you (and I) have energy needs. They will help you understand and align yourself with how energy flows. (I published them in Book 1 on pages 52/53. In case you missed them, here they are again.)

The Rules of Energy Flow

- Good energy flow can be maintained throughout the body with movement and exercise.
- Energy pathways in the body must be open so energy can flow freely. There should be no blockages.
- Energy pathways in the body must be kept clean so energy can flow freely. There should be no toxic substances present.
- Energy flow affects your everyday health and longevity.
- Failure to adhere to the rules of energy flow brings on sickness, disease, and premature death.
- Energy flow affects behavior, which is directly related to the level of conductivity occurring inside the body. Setting aside cultural and societal expectations, if the level of conductivity is good, then behavior will be good. If the level of conductivity is poor, then behavior will be poor.
- Energy needs are defined as energy coming in (food, drink, and other things including energy from other people) and energy going out (expended or simply excess being released, e.g., during exercise). These needs, which are unique to the individual, determine and regulate personal energy flow by monitoring what is required at any given time. For example, when you need more of

something, you'll seek it; when you have too much, you'll find a way to either use it up or release it; when you are exhausted, you'll rest to recharge.
- Proper release and flow are the primary ways to nurture one's wholly integrated self.
- These principles of energy flow are already "known" to each person because they are embedded in the subconscious.

What are Your Energy Needs?
Make a list of the Foundational Energy Elements that are present in your everyday life. How many others are not present? Are the ones there present in a sufficient amount? Do you need to have even more? And for the ones not evident, how can you bring them into your life in sufficient quantity to make a difference?

13

The Need for Energy Safety

*Intuition is always trying to lead you
to a place of safety. Trust it.*

Safety is first on the list of Foundational Energy Elements because it has the highest priority. It is required to protect yourself. To be safe energetically, you need to both *feel* safe and actually *be* safe. Sometimes that can be a tall order.

With all the integration I experienced in 2020, some of the fragments have their own stories to tell. Their stories surface just as my other stories do—they just come. They, too, are healing.

When Home Is Not Safe

My childhood home clearly was not a safe place. Heavy analytical thinking eventually became my "safe place" in my head. With all the fragmentation that had occurred, analytical thinking was pretty much all I had left to work with. Then Dad left. In his will, he left me 25 percent of his estate. Thank you. But years later, I had to fight to receive it.

Both stories—"Legs of Cement" (age 12) and "Thoughts of Suicide at Fifteen" from Book 1—happened before I ever knew fragmentation had occurred. Most of the damage had already been done by the time I was 12. I had no idea the events described in these stories were a sign something was wrong. So was the first epiphany I had at age 12/13, referenced in the next chapter.

I wish I'd known then what I know now. I would have sought help in the form of a counselor.

I wish I'd known then what I know now. I would have sought help in the form of a counselor.

One of the early readers for my first book is a psychologist who told me experiencing cement legs like I did is not all that unusual. I wish I'd known that years ago, too. Instead, I wondered about it for all those years. Safety—physically and energetically. I realize these two stories were both my intuition and my physical body telling me something was wrong. They were trying to protect me.

Your intuition can and will guide you to a place that's emotionally, physically, mentally, and financially safe for you. Know that it may take time—even a lot of time—but it will happen.

Bullying and stonewalling was Mom's customary way of dealing with things. I had to walk on eggshells to avoid triggering that behavior. Pure avoidance worked, too. (If you are experiencing bullying, stonewalling, or walking on eggshells, consider getting counseling.)

Distancing is another useful tool. Divorcing my husband and eventually moving away from Mom and John helped me immensely. But, still, it took years to learn I didn't have any boundaries—with them or with anyone. I wish I'd known long ago that I needed to establish boundaries with people in my life.

So, how do you create safety boundaries? Intentions work.

Building an Energy Protection Wall

People and nations must have strong borders to protect themselves against intruders, persons of ill will, toxic/negative energy, and brainwashing (by others). We are usually not taught how to do this or that we even should.

I had nightmares growing up in the log cabin. In addition, Mom told me that when I was small, she would find me three flights of stairs below my bedroom at the basement/garage door. I was screaming and fighting with the locked door, trying to get out. Yes, that was the same place "Legs of Cement Story" took place years after that!

I wish I'd known what was going on in the house. I wish I'd known I could build for myself an energy wall by using my mind. Of course, Mom herself was a big part of the problem. Certain people in my circle of acquaintances were also a problem. One of them overran others—and one of those who was overrun was me! When my counselor and I discussed this, in an unusual moment, she said that when I figure out how to handle my ex-husband, I'll know how to handle this person. She was right. After talking with a friend who had an ex-husband she had to deal with, I set the intention for building an energy wall. It was exactly what she had done, and it worked. Here's what followed.

I stated I wanted a wall of energy to block my ex-husband (and anyone like him) who was just plain toxic. This energy wall would act like a line in the sand. I waited for an acknowledgment of this, and within a few minutes, I telepathically heard the words, "Are you sure?"

"Yes," I answered.

Within a few more minutes, I sensed a shift in my personal energy field on my left side and out in front of me. Nothing else happened after that until a few weeks after setting the intention. My ex-husband and I attended a Christmas Eve party along with others. At the party, one of the people I had an issue with naturally gave me great distance. Was this my energy wall working? Perhaps!

Then I actually sat across the table from my ex-husband. I didn't have to sit there, but I saw an open chair and said, "Oh, what the hell." I took my plate of food and sat down across from him. No problem. As we chatted, I glanced at my two adult children across the room and saw their looks of astonishment. No worries; we were not rekindling anything. Our conversation was civil, no boundaries were crossed in words or tone, and meaningful comments were made about family members we both knew during our 25 years together.

We chatted during the time it took to eat, then he left and mingled with others, and so did I. That interaction happened in 2019. I have seen none of the people I've had an issue with since. My energy wall worked!

Once built, this personal protective wall can be yours. Protect it. Maintain it well. Refresh it and, from time to time, refine it as you determine *what a boundary should be for* in your life.

Timing Had to Be Right

Safety and timing (see Chapter Fifteen) are two prime reasons I drag my feet. Both my divorce and my "Legs of Cement Story" taught me I could not remain in my childhood home and in my marriage. But I had to stay until leaving happened on my own terms or until the timing was right. After almost 14 years of being away following my divorce, I returned to live in Wisconsin after John had passed. Until then, being in Wisconsin wasn't safe enough. During the times I traveled back around Mom's death and dealing with her estate, I had to be careful. I had been warned my brother was saying things that caused serious concern for my safety. That meant if I were to move back to my home state, I had to wait.

Resources for Getting Help

If you are in any kind of a situation that is a threat to your safety—physical or emotional—leave if you can. Get help. And don't return until it is safe enough to do so. See Recommended Resources at the end of this book.

14

Trust the Epiphanies That Come to You

The cadence along with each word of an epiphany are specific for you.

EPIPHANIES ARE A SPECIAL KIND OF GUIDANCE. MINE gave me courage to do things I didn't know I *needed* to do and *could* do. It was courage I didn't know I had inside. It was waiting for me to find it. In the meantime, until I did, my epiphanies lit the way.

Epiphanies are thoughts that come "out of the blue"—ones we just know are the truth—coming from either deep inside or a higher power. At least, that is how I sensed them.

In this chapter, I describe five of the powerful epiphanies I've experienced. I listened to them. I followed their guidance. Each one was right. Collectively, they changed my life.

I know that epiphanies can be trusted, and I offer these five as validation for that premise.

> ***Epiphany #1***
> 1960 at age 12 (pages 51 and 53 Book 1): My own energy blockages were created early in life, too, but my path was different from theirs (Mom's and my brother's). I had an epiphany that *something was wrong in the house. I didn't know what it was. I just knew it wasn't me.*

Looking back, there was plenty wrong. Within one year, Mom and Dad were divorcing; they had lawyered up and worked out all the details by the fall of 1961. It was up to Mom to pull the trigger, which she did in May 1962. Then she pulled it back. Divorces don't happen overnight; there is usually a slow buildup.

With this as the backdrop to all the fragmentation that had already occurred, no wonder I felt something was wrong in the house!

But something was also wrong with me. I'd reacted. And it hurt me. I developed a chocolate allergy that didn't end until 2001. More than that, I experienced fragmentation that began in infancy and didn't end until 2020. This epiphany was painfully right. Because I trusted it, I began to distance myself from my family. That meant walking a lonely path, but it was the right one.

Epiphany #2

1984 at age 35 (page 83 Book 2): Going back to my hometown was never easy. The first time in 1984, I went kicking and screaming inside. But I also sensed a soft, quiet voice telling me *it's the right thing to do*. That voice was right.

I didn't know where the voice was coming from. Was it the "voice" of one of my fragments that would not return until 2020? Or from some other guidance? Possibly a deceased relative or someone still living? I have not figured that out. Truthfully, it doesn't matter. I just knew that going back was right. So, I listened. It quieted me to simply follow the words. Doing so gave me the emotional support I needed. And it was right, given all that flowed from it—namely, a whole new life—because I found that nothing there had changed.

Epiphany #3

1986 at age 37 (page 119 Book 1): After having moved back to my hometown for two-and-a-half years, *I needed to go to law school in order to become the person I always could have been.*

Little did I know the doors to attending law school would swing open. Little did I know a divorce would follow. Little did I know the writing would follow, too. Today, there is much more coming. I can sense it. Without the writing, none of it would be. Without the divorce, none of it would be. Without the law degree, none of it could follow. Without having gone back to school at the age of 40, my life would be toast. My life *had* been toast, and then it changed. I needed to take matters into my own hands on a legal issue stemming from Dad's estate years earlier. I had to fight.

Epiphany #4
1995 at age 47 (page 177 Book 1): The epiphany to divorce. *So be it and all that flows from it.*

The word divorce had not been in my vocabulary, but it had to emerge. Sitting on the bed one day and hearing his words expressed without emotion left me without a marriage. I filed. I've never looked back. To this day, more than 25 years after that moment, all that flows from it is still flowing... rightly.

Epiphany #5
2001 at age 52 (page 36 Book 1): Regarding my 47-year allergy to chocolate... *I will start to eat chocolate again, and I will be fine.* I heard this and questioned it. Yes, I was indeed fine. My "chocolate" epiphany began releasing the built-up energy I had stored inside since childhood. My allergy ended in 2001.

Because details matter, I wondered why it was chocolate I was allergic to for all those years. Then I began to look at the word itself. It sounds like "chalk a lot" or a lot of teaching. It was the Hershey chocolate bars that had been off limits in Dad's office. Hershey is a city in Pennsylvania with the postal abbreviation PA—for pa, as in father. I see Pennsylvania as the combination of two words: Sylvania, a company that makes light bulbs, and Penn as in writing instruments. I put the two words together and see the light that can come with a pen. Another is Pennsyl, as in pencil. All are references to education. And one more. I see Hershey as a combination of the two words "her" and "she," a reference to strong feminine energy.

Going deep even just for a moment like this can yield answers. These words spoke volumes to me. Internal, deep conversations can be like this—insightful and adding a kind of depth to something that at first appears simple when it is actually complex.

Epiphanies and You
Each word of your epiphany is chosen specifically for *you*. Write it down. Remember it exactly as you heard it. You may never have had an epiphany, but I suspect that once you begin this journey, you will.

At first you won't like it and then you will. These words were guidance that didn't rise to be an epiphany, but they repeatedly had significance. Heed them!

15

Notice Timing Is Critical

*When I drag my feet, more often than not,
it's about timing.*

TIMING IS DEFINED BY *OXFORD DICTIONARY* AS "A particular point or period of time when something happens." Within my discussion of energy, this works as a definition. Timing is a critical element of direction and nurturing, which can come in many forms. Timing gets your attention!

Can you think of a time when an answer to something you wondered about was delivered in an unusual way? It could be overhearing a conversation in an elevator or on a bus; it could be noticing words from the side of a bus, from a billboard, or from a newspaper headline that shout your answer. Be open to these possibilities. Better yet, just be *open*. Guidance, direction, and help of all kinds can come when you are open to receiving them. Trust.

Mom once taught me about listening for the timing that comes from inside. I have never forgotten her words: *wait for the signal*.

Wait for the Signal Story

Mom had said, "Wait for the signal." The moment I heard those words, I knew what she meant. Odd. Because I hadn't heard them before, and they were never explained. Somehow, I just knew.

When I was really young and scared to try anything, Mom and I went to Linn Pier where she set out to teach me how to swim. I listened to her. She showed me by first demonstrating how to do an easy swimming motion—a dog paddle. But before trying it, I waited, just as she told me. I paused until I heard the words. Luckily, she didn't push me to go until I was ready. It didn't take long.

Before long, I had this distinct feeling inside. It was subtle, and I knew. Now . . . go . . . go now. So, I jumped in and dog paddled! She taught me other strokes and then how to dive into the water from the edge of the pier. I was only four years old; official swimming lessons from the local water safety patrol would happen when I was old enough. Once I got going, though, I never looked back.

Many years later when I took up swimming to get back into shape, those words came back to me: "Wait for the signal." I hadn't thought about them for years. This time, while at a fitness center's outdoor swimming pool, I knew I likely couldn't swim even one length. But I had to try.

Getting in the pool felt wonderful as I swam for the first time in a number of years. Eventually reaching the other side of the pool, I stopped to catch my breath. I waited and then swam a bit more, quickly becoming exhausted. But not long after—following a few attempts to swim more than one length—that feeling came back to me. At that point, I was standing at the end of the pool getting ready to go again when I sensed my mother's words: "Wait for the signal."

I waited. I knew that *all of me* had to be "on board" and "ready to do this." If not, I could run out of gas fast and not get very far. That day, I could feel what a difference waiting for the signal made in my drive, in my performance. I swam with determination, perseverance, and a knowing that *I could do this*.

Keep in mind, only a few of the fragments had returned at the time I swam in the outdoor pool. All the rest were waiting to return—waiting for me to look for them when it was their time to return. I had no idea there were more than those first few missing pieces.

If I hadn't waited then, I might have given up.

Writing and publishing my third book, I can see how this lesson has become important today. Timing is critical to delivering its message of hope and peace, to recommend action people can take to help themselves. Often while writing, I simply "wait for the signal." Only then do the words the fragments want to say come to me. The Lumberyard Kids, the Log Cabin Girl, and the Office Girl have much to say that the "old me" wouldn't understand. We do now.

In fact, I find "waiting for the signal" matters in everything I do. Life is better. A peace resides inside where peace couldn't be felt before.

Timing

Nowhere is timing more evident than in a disaster. It's critical you listen and trust that inner voice of truth. Seconds can count. But mostly it's about honoring that feeling or sense of what you *should* do—or not do. Timing protects you. Overall, it's often the vehicle for information to come, ensuring you are in the right place at the right time. Getting information to you is the cornerstone purpose of timing.

Trust should be paramount for everything you do. Glean information from sources you know are truthful but then go one step further—which we don't do often—and ask yourself this: "I know this is what experts are telling me, but what is right for *me*?" Trust and listen for the answer to come. Because it will. Expect it. When it does, ponder it and ask, "Why is *this* the answer? Am I understanding it correctly?"

> *Trust should be paramount for everything you do.*

By asking these questions, *you'll learn about yourself and even see patterns over time.*

Storm Protocols

Protocols are procedures that kick in automatically when danger is detected. People have protocols for dealing with different kinds of emergencies, and that's true for you. Have protocols for yourself so you can face any kind of storm coming your way.

In my view, it could include storms of weather like hurricanes, but also storms of viruses, negative energy, abuse of power, and others. Protocols serve to protect you, your loved ones, your economic livelihood, your community, and your country to provide the best-case scenario for survival. Here is part of what I mean.

Hurricanes: We hear one might be coming our way. We have already prepared by setting aside supplies for a shutdown if one is necessary. We close up (prepare to board up our homes and businesses). We evacuate, if necessary, and return when it's safe to do so. We do the cleanup. And reopen. This danger can take days to pass and the cleanup months and years. But we know the drill.

Viruses: We hear one might be coming our way. We have already prepped with supplies for a shutdown if one is necessary. We close up (shelter in place) and return to normal when it's safe to do so. We do the cleanup (disinfect). And reopen. This danger can take months to pass. Problem: We can't stay closed up so long that it kills the economy we rely on. Our economy must be built to withstand this kind of storm.

Negative energy: We hear one might be coming our way. We have already prepped with supplies for a shutdown (avoidance) if one is necessary. Like a virus, it spreads easily, so it's highly contagious. We can't see it, but we can sense it through its negative moods and hear it with words. It can kill us, our loved ones, and our economy. One of its favorite tactics is to divide and conquer.

Abuse of power (emotional abuse and the trauma it inflicts): We might not know it is coming. We simply respond by closing up our energy system for a while. But we may have to shut it down for a long time and go into Survival Mode. This danger can take years to pass. Once it does, we return to what we could have been when we feel it's safe to do so. We do the cleanup. And we reopen our energy system, if it's not too late. Because this danger can take years to pass, therein lies the overall problem: We can't stay closed up that long. If we do, we only exist; we do not live.

Doing Things in Advance

You may find you do things in advance. An example is purchasing an item you had not planned to but did so because your intuition strongly indicated you should. Over time, you'll find you definitely did need the item. Your intuition was right.

Walk with me on one purchase I'm reliving as I write. I don't know how this story will end, but I sense possibilities here.

The 4-Cup Measuring Cup Story

As I walked into a local department store, it seemed odd to me. I hadn't been in this one for a long time—not since my children were young. Here I was in California, not Wisconsin, but it seemed like the people walking out of the store had a familiar look. A Wisconsin kind of look. Something had drawn me to this store on this day. This urge had been brewing for a while. Finally, I could not ignore it any longer.

After going up the escalator to the second floor, I searched for the kitchen area and a particular appliance. I didn't find it. "Heck, since I'm here, I'll look around!" I could feel my intuition kicking in to check for something I might need immediately or for the journey ahead. Sure enough, I could feel something in the clearance area had my name on it! As I approached, my eyes automatically glued to a glass 4-cup measuring cup. It looked like something Pyrex would make, but the lettering was green (not the usual red) and said Food Network. I knew this cup was coming home with me.

"This has to be a real score since I found it in the clearance section," I thought. However, at checkout, I learned it wasn't on clearance after all. Full price. Normally, I'd say, "Never mind." But my intuition strongly told me this was needed. I swallowed my pride and paid full price. To this day, I have never regretted that purchase. And I still can't fully say why it was needed then or into the future. I only knew it belonged in my kitchen.

At this moment, the measuring cup is sitting in front of me on my desk as I type. A bizarre feeling tells me this glass cup is mine and means something at a deep level. I recall that my grandmother was trained in Austria as a chef before she emigrated to the U.S. That career never came to fruition, but I might be sensing her passion for cooking.

I do a lot of cooking for myself, and how I cook has totally changed over time. I use spices and seasonings in ways that are new and exciting to me. I cook by intuition, relying heavily on spices and seasonings along with color and texture. It is the darndest thing. (I share this because *how you eat* might shift, as it did for me—for the better.) Through my cooking, I am feeding my energy body as much as my physical body. It is far more interesting!

Having this green-lettered glass measuring cup in my kitchen, and subsequently adding a Food Network app for recipes on my iPad, suggests the groundwork is being laid for *something*. I feel daring to share this, knowing its meaning has not yet shown itself. It will.

16

Circuitry, Chakras, and Connections

A counselor once said to me, "Talk until the tears come. Then you know you've hit something that needed to be healed."

But for how Mom and John were and how I reacted, I would not be writing this book. Because there would be nothing to write about. I do believe others have lived some version of my story. You may be one of them. My stories are meant to provide support for you to allow any fragments to return so you can be restored to be the person you always could have been. That intention includes stories like this next one.

Sequel to Finding the Office Girl Story—January 2020

Over the few weeks following her arrival at my condo, I would see her settling in. Then she suddenly disappeared. I suspected she returned to Dad's office in Lake Geneva where I found her. In my mind, I went looking for her there. Yes, that's where she was.

It was January, and the lake was frozen, yet she stood outside in front of Dad's office—suspended in the air as if the balcony were extended for her to stand on it (though it wasn't). I rose to her level to see how she was. I said nothing at first. She was just staring at the frozen lake the same way she stared at it when I first found her. Then words came to me.

"During all that time you spent here at Dad's office, did you know we went to law school?" Her eyes and face lit up! And as I witnessed her reaction, I felt it in my chest—in my heart—at my heart chakra. JOY! It was a simultaneous reaction. I DIDN'T KNOW THIS WAS POSSIBLE! OMG! I believe it meant to her that *her life was not a total loss*. She then returned with me back to the condo.

She never went back to Dad's office again. She was now home.

This is Energy Talking
When fragments are returning, I've learned there will be times when your routines might change, at least for a day or so. For example, as I was writing this chapter, I didn't feel right physically.

For me, writing stirs the pot inside and brings up matters to attend to. Sometimes it is a feeling of heaviness in my chest and sometimes a fullness in my stomach, which causes me to stop eating. This time it was both: stomach fullness one day, chest heaviness the next morning. When this has happened before, I'd pull back and let come whatever wanted to come.

I realize now I was talking to the fragments, recognizing something was separate from me—something that mattered. Today, I said those words to myself again but in this different context.

Sequel to the Lumberyard Kids Story—January 2021

I sat quietly in the living room chair watching the snow falling in Wisconsin's first major snowfall of the winter. I just stared out the window. I could feel the fullness in my chest and knew to just go with it. I spoke the words, "If you need me to sit in this chair all day, I will. I can cancel out my entire day's schedule. I will do that." As soon as I said that, I sensed relief inside.

I not only cleared my calendar for the day. I even cleared it the rest of the week, faintly sensing I'd need that. This was Tuesday morning. My schedule was wide open all the way to Friday night. Once I did that, I could feel an even deeper sigh of relief.

Next came this response from one of the fragments:

Back then I'd feel relief knowing my distress was being recognized. And I am in distress again today. A different kind this time. I am 72 years old, and what do I do now? White nationalists shredded our country. He was the face of it—with enablers, too. It was his way or the highway for many. Sound familiar? I hurt for all the people. Though he brought up issues that had been present for so long.

I wondered which of the fragments was stating this message. After a quick mind scan, the vibration felt familiar. The 10 year old from the Lumberyard Kids.

All these weeks and months since the Lumberyard Kids surfaced, I knew they were integrating. Little things would occur—like where I put my coffee cup on my desk, where I placed my feet under the desk when writing, and where I put my car keys every day. Subtle changes. But this time, it's different. Now she is grieving.

In the story "Sequel to Finding the Office Girl," I knew what to say to the Office Girl. (What each fragment needs to hear to right their rapidly changing dimensional world can be different.) Solemn. Somber. Dark was her mood. I sensed the next words: "Did you know you are a mom?" She immediately lit up! And I cried at such a happy response.

She asked, "How many?" I said two. A boy and a girl. I waited for her to ask more questions. "How old are they?" I told her. She processed all of this with deep reflection.

Did I feel the Lumberyard Girl's vibration of "happy"? Yes, but it was nothing like what I felt with the Office Girl and her joy about law school. I felt it in my chest—but a much more subdued feeling.

Office Girl had needed to hear one thing; Lumberyard Girl needed to hear something else. I think their difference in age and experience (16 years versus 10) was the reason.

Later in the evening, I turned on TV. Distantly I could "hear" the 10 year old say proudly, "I am a mom." And I could still feel her being happy. She hadn't asked me anything else yet. I would wait.

Next morning, I could still feel her presence. And she was still happy. As I read my emails, I noted one from an old high school friend. "What's a high school?" she asked. I explained. (A 10 year old in 1958 wasn't too focused on schooling, I surmised.)

I then asked her, "What happened—why couldn't you go back into the house? Why did you stay away outside? Why did you fragment?"

She replied, "It wasn't a choice. The verbal dismissal from Mom was just too often and too much. Why I didn't tell Dad, I don't know. I should have. It might have ended that and made a difference for me. But I didn't." She then added, "For the others, it was the rubber hose and the other rough treatment. And Mom preferred John. While we all waited for you to return, the others kept asking me, what did we do wrong? I told them I thought they did nothing wrong. It's how they (meaning Mom, Dad, and John) were."

She added one more thing. Being outdoors was a way to escape the dryness of the log cabin. The cracked lips and the nose bleeds during winter made her feel miserable—on top of everything else.

Heartbreaking. But this conversation made a difference inside me. I felt a sense of calmness. I have found when someone gets a long-time burden off their chest, it can make this kind of a difference.

It still seemed important that I cleared my calendar for the rest of the week; I wasn't sure why.

I Just Got Here Story—an Eight-year-old Lumberyard Kid—February 2021

On February 3, 2021, about 10:15 p.m., I walked into the living room from my bedroom. I'd retired about an hour earlier, but I had not fallen asleep yet. Something was bothering me. Things felt odd, and I didn't know why.

Walking into the living room signaled something was definitely going on. On one hand, everything seemed familiar, but on the other, something was totally new. I stood still, grabbed a pad of paper and a pen, and started to write what I sensed.

> Just got here. We've written books? This is the third one? Yikes!!! We are smart. We've done something with this life. It wasn't a total waste. Thank you for telling me. I can sleep now. I am HOME.

I felt a sense of relief inside. And calmness.

That's all I heard from her. But later I heard from another 10 year old (a different Lumberyard Kid than the leader) who told me she was amazed by all of this writing. It seemed they were surfacing at this time, lots of them.

Your Energy System

I realize the title of this chapter is about the energy system, including chakras, meridians, and more. But I believe my stories exemplify your soul's plight without a heavy analysis of the mechanics of the energy system. I leave the discussion of mechanics to others who have documented their findings and simply know more than I do.

Learning about your energy system is a big deal with good and not-so-good information out there. Be careful who you listen to. But for now, let me give you a nudge to look in these directions for yourself.

Chakras and Energy

Chakras are defined as any of several points of physical or spiritual energy in the human body according to yoga philosophy. You have at least seven major chakras in your energetic body. You can check them to know they are spinning—and spinning in the right direction. I first felt a chakra spinning in the palms of my hands, though that's not a major chakra area. I have been told this is a first sign of one's awareness increasing. Don't let it throw you when you begin to feel this; it's a good thing. Later, you won't notice it.

Over time, I learned that my first, second, and third chakras were severely blocked. Energy flows through us like a creek or a river but with one blockage, that river gets dammed and energy has to either flow around it or get built up. That blockage registers either as pain or no pain due to numbness. With my lower three chakras being so blocked, experiencing them open up became a game changer. Yoga helped immensely.

Third Eye and Energy

You have a third eye in the middle of your forehead that's part of your energy system and connects to intuition. Using a sleep mask over your third eye can help you recover from trauma and overuse. It's easy to put your entire energy system on overload in times of uncertainty and when you're relying on your instincts to find your way. Computers provide a parallel to this. When you have too many "windows" open, everything slows down. Close some windows, let the others finish their processing, take a rest, and enjoy quiet time. These all serve to bring everything back up to normal fairly quickly.

Subtle Energies

Subtle energies are extraordinary sensors. Being in Survival Mode likely means they're turned off or at least limiting your access to them. For example, these are the ones that guide you, usually without a word being spoken. They show you in quiet ways that can be easily missed. Such as turning left when you normally go right. Such as choosing this coffee cup versus another. Such as pausing when you enter a room to get a feel for what's happening there. Subtle energies at work for you.

To be 100 percent of who you could always have been, get your subtle shutdown energies turned back on. To be 100 percent of who you could always have been, get your subtle shutdown energies turned back on. As with everything else, there is an order to restoring the energy system of which these sensors are integral. In time, they will turn on without help because, naturally, they are normally turned on.

Aligned with Nature

Years ago, I would have said I was fundamentally in alignment with Nature. But not like I am today. I'm naturally tuned into what is happening with the weather (that can be a safety issue). I notice when the wind picks up (often a cue to do something). I eat heavier foods about a week before a major snowstorm (with its frigid temperatures). This sensation feels innately tied to my survival. I haven't had to work at this, and you won't either.

Aligning with Nature happens naturally as you begin to recover and become restored.

Other Circuits and Issues

At the beginning of this journey, it didn't take long to feel energy shoot out my feet. Sounds weird, I know. I didn't see the energy, but I sure could feel it.

As circuits inside you get unblocked and allow your natural energy to flow downstream again, you might also notice and feel oddball things. For example, I had a lot of navel and head activity during the night and especially in the early morning hours. This means change is happening.

During the night is a prime time for your body's energy system to do its repair work. I became aware of this many times over the recent years. It reminds me of highway construction work done at night in low traffic time when repairs can be done more quickly than in the day.

The following story provides an example of an impediment to an energy circuit.

The Letter "L" Story

In first grade, I had a speech defect. One day while playing on the playground during recess, one of my classmates turned to me and said, "You talk funny." Bless her heart, she then took my hand and marched me into our classroom where our teacher was sitting behind her desk. My teacher asked me a few questions and quickly picked up on the problem: how I pronounced the letter "L."

Normally when you pronounce that letter, your tongue touches the roof of your mouth. I wasn't doing that, and I could hardly hear the difference when the teacher had me do it correctly. Finally, I learned to move my tongue in the right way. However, when I'm tired, I can revert to not doing it right.

Over the years, I have figured out the roof of your mouth is an important place for energy to flow from your head. Touching it with your tongue is necessary, because it promotes good energy flow from inside the skull cavity and your highly active brain. So, to me something as simple as a speech defect can have greater importance than is commonly acknowledged. That touch provides a key energy connection.

17

EnergySpeak—The Language of Life

Life's as easy as A-B-C and 1-2-3.

ENERGYSPEAK IS A TRANSLATION OF SORTS. I'VE called it WordPlay in my first two books and am further developing it here. Words have an energy root to them. By understanding the meaning at that fundamental level of energy, you can gain insights about a word's deeper meaning. This is the level of EnergySpeak. It can be convoluted at times and even slippery—but insightful, fun, and deeply rewarding.

Soul/Sole/So-UL/So-u-L

Ever notice the two words soul and sole? Sole refers to the bottom of your foot; you can't see it but, in effect, you stand on it. So-UL. When I first noticed this, "So" was clear to me but the "UL" part? Yet, it looked familiar. Oh yes, Underwriter's Laboratory—UL—is a tag on every electrical appliance we purchase. UL means electrical. "So electrical." Yes, that would be us.

Then there is So-u-L. The letter L refers to me as if to call me L (Elle). The movie *Legally Blonde* came to mind in the main character Elle Woods. Intuition was her thing. Mine, too. At the time I watched that movie, my fragments were still fragments. But in a way, this was telling me my writings were "so me."

Morning/Mourning

Ever notice the similarity between these two words? The difference in their spelling is the letter "u." Mourning starts with a reference about "darkest before dawn" or grief. When the light begins to return, it's the dawning of a new day. Thus, morning follows mourning.

Butt/But

Saying you'd like to do something, *but* . . . is the same as sitting on your *butt*. Nothing happens.

Peephole/People

Just as we say the poet's eyes are the window to the soul, when

I hear the word "people," I hear the word "peephole." Its human form is "housing for the soul." That's why it matters that you learn what you really are made of—energy.

Responsibility
About the word "responsibility," in Book 2 on page 56 I wrote: "We normally use this word to refer to a person's ability to be responsible." That is true, but like a lot of things, we rarely look deeply enough for what it relates to. "Responsibility" relates to a person's ability to respond—namely, to respond to one's circumstances. For some (including me for years), that ability to respond is diminished due to Survival Mode.

Glass Half Full or Glass Half Empty
If your glass is half full or half empty, it could mean YOU are only half present.

Depression
Soul sadness. Think of weather and how we use terms such as "it's a low, not a fair-weather high" or "it's a tropical depression." It implies energy suppression is occurring on the soul itself and that someone is likely not being true to him/herself.

Wail/Whale
A "whale" that swims in our oceans can energetically symbolize our personal "wail" of emotional pain that gets stuck/lodged in our energetic field. A whale swims and exists often undetected in the electromagnetic ocean of this planet. It can also relate to our

subconscious mind (a whale) where our emotional pain (wail) resides unnoticed.

A-B-C and 1-2-3

The quotation for this chapter came to me early after my chocolate release. A-B-C is about words, the alphabet, and paying attention. A for Always; B for Be; C for Clean. It can refer to washing your hands and having clean water to do it, which is about safety—personal safety. This isn't about cleanliness only during pandemic times; it's about cleanliness always.

Always Be Clear is another version that can go a long way to getting what you want, knowing how you want to be treated, and avoiding misunderstandings. That applies to intentions, too.

When striking out is not the immediate issue, then 1-2-3 refers to learning about your patterns. *You'll be more kind to yourself once you realize it may take one, two, or even three tries to get something to work right.* However, watch out. We often keep pounding at the same thing when we need to move on instead. This is true for making ourselves "fit in" to be someone we are not. Solutions may not be clear at first, but if you are watching for your 1-2-3 pattern, you'll quickly know what is right for you.

18

What Feeds Your Soul

*You are all one person. Peace comes when
your fragments return home.*

As I've gone through my many changes during this journey to become the person I always could have been, I've realized what feeds my Soul is Home, is having my Energy and Physical Together, and yet understanding they—the Energy and Physical—are Still Divided (because it takes time to merge). These are three of the realizations I've discovered about what feeds my Soul. I am certain there are more. Let me further explain these.

1) HOME

Home. Your family, your physical body, your country can all be labeled Home. But bringing back any fragments IS bringing you Home—to your energy body, to your "heart," to the rest of your soul that is waiting to receive those fragments.

Home. It should be a safe place. Everyone should *feel* and *be* safe at Home. As you have learned, Emotional Abuse is an Abuse of Power that causes severe energy reactions within the Soul. Reactions can include fragmentation, allergy, and dissociation. Survival Mode can result.

Based on my experience, bringing back your fragments is paramount to ending Survival Mode and facilitating your recovery energy-wise. With the pieces united, your whole person can be present and functioning fully—or at least closer to 100 percent.

Bacon. Since the release of my chocolate allergy, every time I went to the grocery store, I purchased bacon. Well, maybe not *every* time, but close! When I'd walk past the area where the prepackaged bacon was displayed, my eyeballs would immediately lock on one of the packages. Sometimes hickory smoked, sometimes applewood smoked, sometimes not smoked at all—different brands, different thicknesses, and different ... you name it! They all found a way into my refrigerator. But perhaps it went beyond the characteristics of aroma, sizzle, and taste.

Not until 2020 did I figure out many of my energy needs. Bacon was among them. Why? It's related to the old saying *bringing home the bacon*. That means bringing home the money you want to have in your bank account, which references discovering your energy needs. Realizing what your needs are and supporting them to the fullest will get you there.

What's that got to do with actual bacon? Hear me out in this story.

Bringing Home the Bacon Story

Saturday night, February 3rd, 2001. I began to eat chocolate again after a 47-year absence due to an anaphylaxis allergy discovered when I was six. Following my intuition that "I'd be fine," I ate chocolate sparingly every day for the next five days. On the sixth day—Friday, February 9th—I had a wild experience that shook me. The "Crystal Coffin Story" in Book 1 relates the full experience, but that wasn't the end of it. (I wasn't good at linking events at that point in my life.) The "Legs of Cement Story" (also in Book 1) detailed another energy experience when I was 12. These two events marked "frozen" legs and "frozen" physical body years later. With my body frozen, I could only move my eyes. Both frozen occurrences released on their own after a short time, but in both cases, my soul was releasing energy for a reason. At age 12, being frozen prevented me from going back into the log cabin (at least for a few moments) and signaled something was wrong. As part of the chocolate allergy ending and being able to eat chocolate, my body didn't know what to do with all the energy. So, on that sixth day, it did an "emergency blow"—that is, a good chunk of the real me surfaced after being suppressed for all those years. Immediately, I needed massages to further facilitate this energy shift. From that, I learned to never underestimate the power of one's soul.

Now to explain the bacon.

In 2001, I was still in full Survival Mode, but change was happening. As I said earlier, I began purchasing bacon almost every time I went for groceries. It clearly was important to have some bacon cooked and some in the freezer to enjoy anytime I wanted it.

When I was growing up, Mom did not cook bacon with the exception of Canadian bacon for my dad. (That kind of bacon is good but not the same as the kind I'm referencing. I want to have *real* bacon.) I would cook an entire package on a weekend and then wrap it in a paper towel, place it in a plastic bag, and freeze it all. Every time I sensed I wanted to eat some, I'd pop it in the microwave for a few seconds and chow down. Magic!

Purchasing the bacon with my own money, cooking it for only me, and using my freezer to hold it until I wanted to give myself an energy/protein boost send a clear message to my mind and to the Universe. Today, I'm aware that writing is my way of "bringing home the bacon" for myself, my family, and those I hope to help.

2) ENERGY AND PHYSICAL TOGETHER

Feeding the soul needs to happen at both the energy level and the physical level. Engaging my mind to support the soul's work using associations while nourishing the physical at the same time has worked well.

I found these combinations of food and intention especially worked well together:

- I craved beef when I was processing a "beef" I had with someone. It could be about something that happened years ago or just yesterday. That person may be alive or gone, it didn't matter. It was a "beef" that needed my attention. So, with every bite, every chew, I knew I was disintegrating the "beef" until it was gone.

- I craved chicken when I was processing "being chicken"—meaning being scared of something or someone. Again, with every bite, every chew, I shredded the food. Imagine standing at the grocery store looking over which "chicken" to purchase while knowing it's about energetically recognizing your fear and calling it out for what it is—chicken. Yellow. Scared. Afraid. Terrified. Many times, I've had to do this. It has worked.

Eventually, I craved beef and chicken less. Today, when I want beef, it feels like "I'm beefing up now"—getting stronger. And now when I want to eat chicken, my word for it is "poultry," which sounds like pole-try or "I'll try."

The foods listed here helped educate and encourage me in different ways.

Chocolate—reminded me I had something I would be teaching. "Chalk" a-lot of it.

Fish—added flow to my energy system.

Catsup (ketchup)—signaled it was time to "catch up!" I'm behind.

Molasses—reminded me I was being too slow.

Eggs—I craved eggs to get the eggshells for processing my feelings after "walking on eggshells." I'd grind them up in the garbage disposal. Done.

Of course, I could list many others, with each one targeting some area of my life that needed clearing. As strange as these food references might sound, being aware of them has made a difference.

Remember the list of the Foundational Elements of Energy from Chapter Twelve including Grounding and Variety? Here is an example of how many of them can apply in everyday situations.

Making My Beef Stew Story

My mission: To process a "beef" and feel a sense of grounding.

Because I knew my grocery stores (five in my area), deciding which one to go to for the beef started the process. Following my intuition led me to something "on special," a person behind the counter I could chat with, and other items I needed. Determining what the selected store offers versus the other four became part of the equation as well. All without me knowing anything to start with except which store to go to. This is an expression of Variety.

The first stew I made used chunks of beef sirloin—purchased on sale—plus carrots, rutabaga, parsnip, onion, and frozen peas.

Once I selected the beef, I had to find parsnips, which I'd never used before. No problem. With each item, I could tell my eyes were carefully selecting which bag of peas, which bunch of carrots, which rutabaga, which kind of onion (white, yellow, shallot), and which one of the parsnips to bring home. Quite a process. I had to remind myself, "This is not only about making a beef stew. It's about *stewing my beef* and getting *good grounding* from the root vegetables provided by the earth and a farmer."

Once home, I created a beef bouillon broth with seasonings—two or three kinds of salt and pepper, basil, parsley—and anything else I wanted. I noticed:

Texture includes the shapes of the meat, the vegetables (how I cut them), the salt and pepper, and the flakes of the dried herbs.

Color is obvious to find, given what went into this stew.

Scent refers to the aroma of the stew simmering on the stove and later on my plate.

Sound is heard in the grocery store, in chopping vegetables, in unwrapping meat. I'm playing music when I am alone and cooking, or I hear the sound of others' voices when they are present as we all cook. (The sizzling sound of bacon when it cooks is tough to match!)

Taste—is obvious and usually delicious.

Movement—refers to physical body movements when preparing the dish, stirring the stew, and seeing everything come together—even dancing in the kitchen between chores.

Realizing you're incorporating your energy into the dish you are creating is important. Touching the food, stirring it, and looking at the meals you make for yourself (and others) transfer your energy into it.

What about baking? Bread, cookies, pastries, pies—just so goooood! My favorite "go-to" treat is cookies. What kind, which ingredients? Again, all the energy elements come into play. Crispy or smooth cookies? Raisins? Chocolate? The choices are endless, and I have found them all to be healing. My freezer likes being filled with desserts; my waistline does not. But I have found when recovering from reactions to emotional abuse (or anything else such as the stomach flu), it's common to eat differently because of physical and energetic requirements.

And one more. When I want to process "money matters," I create "dough" (as in pie dough). The rolling pin feels great in my hands—like it could be used as a weapon. Pie weights for baking a pie shell are just so cool, too! I roll out the dough and make a whole pie that only I own.

For some time, I have felt something was wrong as I acknowledged the many insidious ways Survival Mode can affect one's life. Yes, the pain of emotional abuse shows up in many ways including what we ingest. Looking back, my digestion played a major part of my Survival Mode response. Chocolate and a lack of digestive fire were two primary ways I was shut down. They were part of my reaction. So were many more elements. Hydration. Fats/oils. Breathing. Posture. Being sedentary. All mine, too.

If you want to get rid of Survival Mode and gain percentage points fast, identify your Survival Mode response and do your

If you want to get rid of Survival Mode and gain percentage points fast, identify your Survival Mode response and do your best to release it and/or reverse it. Take off the brakes to reveal You—your true self.

best to release it and/or reverse it. Take off the brakes to reveal You—your true self.

What also helps? Creating an internal environment that is necessary for you to grow—to become the person you always could have been. Any Foundational Energy Elements that have been missing will naturally reveal themselves when you trust and listen to your intuition. Consider these key elements:

Hydration: I never drank enough liquids. As reported, much of the U.S. population experiences dehydration, which affects internal energy flow. Fluids are a stream. Without them, energy tries to flow over a dry riverbed. But that doesn't work. Drink water, a lot of it. As I have been guided to understand: *At first you won't like this, and then you will.*

Posture: Mom used to threaten to put me in a harness because I wouldn't stand up straight. (She never did.) But I did nothing; to me, it wasn't that bad. Today, I know that posture affects digestion and breathing. And digestion needs room. Even the slightest slouch compresses that area of your body, which can affect your internal efficiency. It can also give the appearance of *not fully standing up for yourself.*

Fats/Oils: Highly necessary for full functioning. Organic and high grade oils are the key to effective energy transmission throughout your body—both your energy and physical bodies. For me, a tablespoon of coconut oil every day in my morning coffee works to hydrate and lubricate.

Chocolate: A direct link to Dad and his log cabin office, also my being more like him and not emulating my mother. Chocolate releases emotion and aids in digestion. I had no voice back then. I am gaining it now.

Breathing: Belly (deep) versus chest (shallow). Many people are shallow breathers, which is not helpful inside. In fact, it serves to suffocate. When you get scared, do you breathe in a shallow way? I suspect you do. I did. I found I could correct that by intentionally breathing down toward my pelvic floor, so my breath reaches my belly. I also found any fear subsided immediately with the breath change. But old habits can be hard to break, and shallow breathing can return easily. Be aware of it and retrain yourself. Your body needs the oxygen.

Movement: Exercise of any kind is good for the outside of the body—and the inside. That's why we call a walk after eating a meal a "daily constitutional." Movement is foundational. Yoga, tai chi, massage, acupuncture, and more. These move energy, too.

Heat: As a general rule, warm your food and drinks. It means a little less digestive work for you inside. Heating what you take in is thoughtful, too. You likely wouldn't serve a guest food that is cold—so don't do that for yourself, either.

Digestive Fire: It may be lacking in your belly as it certainly was in mine. Welcome Spices and Seasonings!! This was why, right after my chocolate release in 2001, I stacked spices and seasonings on my kitchen counter and opened the silverware chest for a show of force. That was 20 years ago. I had no idea how bad my situation inside was at the time. With everything else that had to be fixed, adding digestive fire had to wait. That addition would happen in an orderly manner. It came in 2020, and it has worked beyond belief. Cardamon, cinnamon, coriander, cumin. These and many other spices have changed my digestive world. (Mom did not use these because of Dad's condition, so I didn't experience them growing up.)

The importance of who cooks your food cannot be overstated.

The importance of who cooks your food cannot be overstated. Because cooks choose what will be served and they make the food, they have the ability to prepare meals that keep their own percentages in place—and the percentages of the others they cook for. I grew up with a cook, my mom, who was 15 percent of who she could have been. When 15 percent people make food for themselves and others, therein can lie energy problems.

Likely no one in a family that dines together is at 100 percent. Possibly that's why people keep a certain level of Survival Mode within their families. Food is one of the primary reasons, plus the energy of others feeds the Survival Mode reaction. The goal is to all get along, but Survival Mode serves to keep everyone in one place.

I'm reminded of the 1990 movie *The Hunt for Red October* at the point when the saboteur was discovered. It took me a long time to figure out why I pinged at that dramatic moment. This movie is about a Russian submarine and its captain who wishes to defect from Russia. After realizing there was a saboteur on board, the captain (played by Sean Connery) discovered who it was—"It's the cook. The damn cook!" Ping! The movie portrayed the cook as an intentional saboteur. I doubt if my mother cooked to be an *intentional* anything. But each of us should consider the role the "cook" in life plays. Who cooks your food?

3) YET STILL DIVIDED AFTER ALL THIS TIME

Once fragments return to one's body, it takes time for them to be restored. *Lots* of time. Those that returned during the writing of this book are still integrating and growing—and it's been an entire year to this point. I sense full integration will take even longer.

Once they've returned, can fragments split off again? Yes, I think they can. It was a coping mechanism back then, and it can be again. Therefore, it's my responsibility to nurture myself, to gain strength, wisdom, and self-protection so pieces of "me" won't need to fragment again. They're home. That is true for you, too, so pay detailed attention to your own self-care.

And for the person I always could have been, my recent journaling tells me it'll take another eight to ten years to get all the pieces back into place. That's because my Survival Mode went on for so long. I suggest you don't let your Survival Mode persist.

19

What You Don't *Know* Can Be the Problem

The most important thing is what you believe.
It affects everything you say and do.

JUST HOW WEAKENED INSIDE YOU ARE CAN BE THE ROOT of your problem, for that's an energy problem. It was certainly my problem. And *increasing* your energy is the solution for it.

So, how do you process and handle all the things coming your way? Adopting these beliefs can help you keep things in perspective:

- You don't need to know everything.

- You only need to know what you need to know.
- You only need to know what to do next.

Reinforcing these thoughts has helped me out of predicaments every step of the way. They continue to do so during the dark times. Integrating these three beliefs can both calm you and give you guidance. They will naturally invoke your own trust.

What you know (or think you know) is a lot, but what you *don't* know is vast and infinite. You might tend to ignore this fact—and you should not.

Survival Mode blocks a lot of what you need to know to grow because its sole purpose is to keep you safe so you live another day. Ending Survival Mode will likely challenge you with the very circumstances you originally found yourself in—situations that caused you to react the way you did. There's a good chance you'll face a fight ahead, perhaps only inside of you. But it may be outside of you (like my fight with my brother), so prepare for it.

Let me share what happened to me years ago—my engagement—and what I didn't know about myself back then. Perhaps you can relate to it.

My Christmas Eve Engagement Story

On Christmas Eve 1969, my now-ex-husband gave me the engagement ring we had picked out earlier and asked me if I still wanted to get married. Where and when that conversation occurred—in the log cabin after everyone had gone to bed—

speaks volumes to me now. I was still up with my bedroom lights on. Only he, Mom, John, and I were in the house. Dad had died four years earlier.

I was sitting fully dressed on the floor of my bedroom when he quietly knocked on the door. Looking back, that is where I was emotionally—still on the floor in my childhood bedroom. At 21, I had some college under my belt, but I had no particular career plans. Adrift.

He asked. I said yes.

The symbolism of sitting on the floor in my childhood bedroom said it all. *I hadn't left my room yet. It had always been my sanctuary. I was still there.* This kind of change would take a lot more than an engagement ring. It would take years. Knowing what I know *now* about myself, what I didn't know *then* mattered a lot.

If you could go back and change something in your past—a moment that could have been informed by what you know now—would you make that change? What would it be and why?

Speaking on another level, a family should be safe, but often it isn't. The "Breaking into the Family Safe Story" in Chapter Three has deep meaning not to be missed about what I *didn't* know and how it mattered.

In the story, I was breaking into an actual safe, but I was also breaking back into the family as a place of safety. After all, this was Dad's safe. I had been part of this family all along but felt like an outsider. Finally, I was breaking into it. As I turned the combination dial this way and that, I realized the real emergency belonged to me; I didn't know just how important it was to feel safe. Both safety of the heart and this actual safe represented Dad's world.

I had trusted my mother and brother at a time I should not have, because they didn't keep me safe. Mom led the way and John followed. Always generous, Dad would never have treated me the way they did.

Growing up in the Midwest, my natural disposition was to trust others and accept what I was told as the truth. After all, why would someone lie? But people do lie. You'll understand this if you have been lied to by someone you would naturally trust such as a parent, a sibling, or a husband. From them, untruths could wash over you, and you'd accept them as true without question. No red flags go off. Like me, you were likely conditioned to accept whatever you're told. Your vulnerability to lies is caused by being in some measure of Survival Mode. Therefore, learning to trust yourself can be a problem. In many subtle and not-so-subtle ways, you might have been taught not to trust yourself. This isn't right.

Again, listening to your intuition helps. When your ability to feel your emotions—and feel safe—return to their optimal functioning level, you'll naturally discern when something is not right. And that discernment will happen more quickly.

20

Learn to Journal and Meditate

Deep inside, you have a voice. Allow it to speak.

GOING DEEP INSIDE AND ASKING QUESTIONS ABOUT *anything* is tantamount to "stirring a pot." It is a good "stir," even if it causes you to relive painful events. Know there's always a good reason behind why that particular question was asked or why that subject was approached.

Journaling is analogous to cleaning out a basement or a garage. Finally, it's done. And who knows what treasures you'll find there! In Book 2, the chapter "Ways to Communicate with Your Inner Self" addresses the basics of journaling, meditation, and other internal communications such as epiphanies, visions, and dreams. If you haven't read it yet, I invite you to take a look. This chapter gives you a deeper sense of what "stirring a pot" does.

It was my journaling and meditation that facilitated the 2001 release from my chocolate allergy. In 1997, early in my growth process, I began routinely doing both. It was in 2001 (not long after I began eating chocolate again) that I pulled out my blue sleeping bag. I had taken it with me when I left my marriage. The sleeping bag itself could be zipped to another similar one so two people could sleep together. We had purchased two of them early in our marriage so we could go snow camping in winter. Which we never did.

The allergy release caused a major shift inside me. I didn't know this sleeping bag would be an important part of this shift. By taking it with me—wanting my half—I realized I was making a statement to the Universe: *We aren't zippered together anymore.* I slept in this bag for several nights after the allergy ended. And I realize it was critically important for other reasons as well.

The Blue Sleeping Bag Story

February 2001. It was hanging on a large hanger in my closet and had been since the divorce. Practically brand new. I pulled it out and had this feeling to put it on my bed on top of the bedspread. That night, I crawled into the sleeping bag and zipped it up to feel nice and snuggled in. No blankets necessary.

The blue sleeping bag. I apparently needed it. Trusting my intuition, I slept with the front door of my second-floor apartment unlocked for at least three nights. Although I grew up with every door locked at night in the log cabin, I sensed an unlocked door would be fine. I also left my bedroom door unlocked and wide open. Both were startling changes for me. I was meant to break out of the "cage" of doing everything the way I had been trained. At least that's what I sensed I needed to do.

Another important part to this scene were the colors of the sleeping bag—medium blue with a small amount of red trim. Odd. Not sure why, but as I crawled into my sleeping bag that first night, it seemed like the blue sky was protecting me. I slept well.

Due to my chocolate release, things happened that were heavy on the spiritual side and needed to be taken seriously. I listened, and I followed. I cleared my dresser of everything except the clear glass vase with its gentle curves. I opened the drawers to shove everything else (except my wristwatch) into them and out of sight. I picked up the watch and delicately lowered it into the clear glass vase as the words to Jim Croce's song played in my head: "If I could save time in a bottle, the first thing that I'd like to do . . ." I knew the bottle in the song was this vase.

I took down wall hangings in my apartment and turned pictured faces toward the wall. I knew my cactus plant had to go. So did a small potted tree. I moved the bed itself so the headboard would be near the window. This would give me an exposure with lots of sunlight in the morning. Apparently, sunshine was needed. The watch stayed in the vase for several weeks. I gradually ate lots of chocolate over the coming days.

And then there was shopping, lots of it, over the days and weeks that followed.

All of this internal energy came on like a firehose. My journaling, meditation, and counseling had facilitated this shift. I was emerging from dissociation. My divorce was five years behind me, yet I could still see it in my rearview mirror.

Guided by meditating and journaling, all this truly stirred the pot inside. And over the years, I grew. Life is different now. For your journey, a quiet space with a lit candle is a good way to start. Fragments, if you have any, like that.

21

What to Say to Others and What They Might Say to You

There may be words waiting to be said that will help you on your way. And what words will you say to others so you can move forward?

OTHERS. THEY MAY WANT YOU TO LOOK TO THEM for all your answers. What to do and what to say? They may be in the habit of informing you (directly or indirectly) that they know more than you do. Churches, authoritarian parents, and others—often well-meaning people—customarily do this. It has been like this for a long time. But that habit may be based on Survival Mode being present. Survival Mode leaves the door open for being extremely compliant.

Those around you may not "get" any of what you are experiencing, so explain to them the best you can. If you feel strongly about something, say so with emotion. They will get that.

Always consider the source of your information, be it scientific or not. And be careful which people you listen to. Is what they say truthful? Does it resonate as being true for you from the inside? Or does their information somehow go against the grain for you?

Remember the old saying: *You can lead a horse to water, but you can't make it drink.* Remember, too: *No one has walked in your shoes, and you've not walked in theirs.* Both of these sayings allow for respectful distances to exist when dealing with others. Heed those distances.

What They Might Say to You

As people hear your story about what you've been through (as much as you care to share), they might make statements that can be life-changing—in a good way. Truth. Compassion. Empathy. Sympathy. Love. These convey healing energy. Soul will love it!

Words and statements from others have both broken me and helped me—things I didn't know but definitely needed to hear. Here are a few things I heard or learned that stand out (shown in bold).

> **It wasn't your fault.** This was said to me at the nursing home regarding Mom and her condition.

I'm so sorry. Also said at the nursing home regarding Mom, and it felt like a salve was being smoothed onto an open wound. That was the first time. But by the fifth or sixth time I heard it, just how bad the situation was began to sink in.

The best thing you could have done was to leave them (Mom and John). Thankfully, I left them emotionally and physically a full year before Mom died.

Let's just say this wasn't the county judiciary's finest hour. This referred to the 1976 closing of my father's estate and the embezzlement by my mother that the court missed.

The pain will go away, but you'll never forget. Said to me in counseling about what I went through during Mom's last few years. It was both consoling and true—that you never forget what happened, all the ugliness. This was another point of realizing how bad the situation was.

The nurse the county sent to help turned out to be a psychiatric nurse. This was when Mom was bedridden but still in the log cabin. Knowing a nurse was coming gave me a measure of relief, but later when I found out she was a psychiatric nurse, it raised a big flag. Mom's health was dire.

This was the worst case of isolation we have ever seen. When we do see it, it usually is between a husband and wife. This was the first time we have seen it between a mother and a son. This was told to me by a county social services worker while Mom was still in the log cabin almost two years before she died.

He hurt her. ("He" referred to John; "her" referred to Mom.) The nurse at Mom's nursing home made this statement, summarizing her conclusion after reading the list of Mom's ailments.

During the audit of Mom's estate, the IRS asked for all the court and medical records from Mom's guardianship hearings. The court released all except the medical records, which it had sealed. For me, this confirmed the extreme seriousness of her health issues that the court didn't want known publicly.

I learned *trust* by listening—not to others but to that little voice inside that said, "It's the right thing to do." If I hadn't, I wouldn't have grown, I wouldn't have learned a damn thing about myself and about others in my life. Glad I listened.

Your first steps are to listen and trust as you dismantle any Survival Mode that's present.

What words are waiting to be said to you to help you along your way?

22

Tell Your Story With Universal Rules of Energy in Mind

*To draw water from a well that is deep in the ground,
the hand pump first needs to be primed.
Journaling, meditation, and counseling each serve
to do this, so you can tell your story.*

YOUR STORY MAY ONLY BE PERSONAL FOR YOU *AND* IT may be worth telling—to both yourself and others. My approach is based on this mantra: *Write whatever you want to say then decide what parts of your writing others would want to know.*

As you write your stories, keep in mind these universal rules of energy.

- Do no harm.
- Do Unto Others As You Would Have Them Do Unto You. (The Golden Rule)
- It's imperative that you meet your foundational energy needs.
- Time as we know it does not exist on the other side. Only *now* exists. That creates an opportunity in *this* time and space for all kinds of energetic recovery.

I can't imagine not having written my story, given what I know now about myself. But what if you have more to your story than you realize? What if it would help others at a community, regional, or national level? I was once told at a writer's conference "the more personal your story is, the more universal it is." That rule has guided me every step of the way.

Of course, writing about yourself is a deeply personal decision only you can make; the same is true about telling others. And deciding to do so is not easy. It starts with seeking to understand the vulnerability that emotional abuse can cause. This story shows what I mean.

The Chevy, Workhorse, and Sting Story

My dad drove Cadillacs. My mother drove Chevys. At least that is how it was when I was growing up. She felt comfortable at that economic level; Dad was not a "Chevy."

Early on, I apparently molded myself after Mom. And little did I know what kind of a life that would lead to. I'd be a workhorse trained to be submissive like her, which meant I was vulnerable to control by others. I did not know this was intended to be almost a life sentence.

Here's an example of that submissiveness for me. During my college years, I was sitting with the man I was dating (and whom I later married) on a sofa in my dormitory lounge. A proctor was present, making sure everyone behaved properly. However, we were sitting where the proctor didn't see what was about to take place.

We'd been dating for a while but no sex yet. In fact, I had done nothing sexually with anyone. That evening, I could feel his penis through his pants. I voluntarily put my head in his lap, not thinking about what might happen next. Once his pants were unzipped and it was in my mouth, I still didn't realize what would happen next because I had never done this before. Then I felt his penis stiffen. I tried to pull back, but he'd placed his hands on the back of my head to hold my head down. Only when my mouth filled with semen did I pull away. In that moment, I should have spit it back in his face. But that wasn't who I was back then. "Submissive me" simply got up and walked to the bathroom to spit it all out. I had no words.

My conclusion? From that point on, he knew I would tolerate behavior like this from him—that I could be controlled.

Months later, still dating, we drove in my car to the log cabin. Yes, I had a Chevy, and he was driving it that day. I remember we parked in the driveway where Mom always parked her car, not Dad's driveway on the other side of the house. After the visit, we walked together to the car and reached my side—the passenger side—first. I stopped, expecting him to open the car door for me. He didn't. He kept walking around to the driver's side. "Why aren't you opening the car door for me?" I asked. I will never forget his response. "You are perfectly capable of opening the car door yourself." I didn't like his answer, but I overlooked it and simply opened the door for myself.

This proved to be a watershed moment in our relationship. From then on throughout our subsequent 25 years of marriage, this attitude prevailed. I had been trained as a workhorse to accept whatever he did—or didn't do. It defined my role, and it set internal boundaries within the relationship.

In a third incident early in our relationship, I felt a sting like a pin prick in my chest, the heart chakra area, every time I thought of him. A kind of warm response in my chest began with this sting and spiraled outward. What was that? I thought the warmth was good, not realizing the full effect of the stinging feeling.

Looking back, the sting felt like I had been harpooned in the heart chakra. I didn't know that was possible. In my view, it was an exploitation of the unprocessed grief and losses I'd experienced until then, and it resulted in extreme emotional vulnerability. Did he consciously know he was doing this? Likely not. But at some deep level, I'd say yes.

Unknowingly, I was operating at about 10 to 15 percent at that time.

Many times, there were no words. Often in my process of healing, I would stand speechless, staring out a window, at a wall of the room I was in, or at the ceiling. Just staring. Sometimes I stared just for a few minutes; other times for several hours. I always felt better afterwards as words would finally come and bring a fresh perspective.

Today, I know my fragmented parts were speaking to me. That's why working with energy is key; it's how the fragments speak to you, too. At first, there are no words—because what happened to them often happened *before* they'd learned to speak.

Without words, those parts (which ranged from infant to 16 years old in my case) will send messages to you using everything around you—signs, visions, epiphanies, dreams, words out of context. *Anything* can symbolize something they want you to know. Part of what makes up your intuition are those lost fragments. They have stories they want you to know and perhaps tell others.

When you journal about your life, you are processing. When it's time to share your whole story with others, if you feel you have to use a pen name, then do so. For me, using a pen name just seemed dishonest. One of my children expressed a strong desire that I do so, but I declined.

In fact, my adult children weren't big on the idea of me writing my story at all, so I held back. I didn't share with them the details about both the writing and the publishing of my first book. *But at some point, you just can't hold back anymore.* Eventually, I gave my daughter and son their copies of Books 1 and 2, and I told them to do whatever they wanted with them. At least I knew they had *their* copies, which was important to me. As my son was leaving with the two books in his hand, I heard him state he would read them. That is his decision to make, *and* it was certainly nice for me to hear.

When I wrote Books 1 and 2, I deliberately chose to not use my children's names or include stories about them. The narrative is about what happened to me; it's what *I* needed to write. They have stories of their own to write!

Now, as my fragments have come together, I visualize them joining hands. They stand together to fight the effects of what abuse can do to a person of any age. So will yours.

And mine will stand with yours!

23

Peace Begins on the Inside and Nowhere Else

*The problem isn't that there is division
in our government; it's that our government
reflects the division we have inside us.
Emotional Abuse does this.
Emotional Abuse is ultimately Abuse of Power.*

IN THE INTRODUCTION, I STATED I HAD SENSED MY LOG cabin experience could present a level of lessons that could be applied to a much larger universal situation. Let me explain.

Overall, my Survival Mode reaction included eczema, an allergy to chocolate (any kind of chocolate), dissociation, fragmentation, a weak digestive fire, sluggish digestion, some constipation, poor hydration, poor posture, shallow breathing, dumbing down, keeping my mouth shut, not taking risks, living a sedentary lifestyle as a child, heavy analytical thinking, not showing a lot of emotion, grieving that went unprocessed, having no boundaries, being too nice, having a speech defect as a child (couldn't enunciate the letter L), sucking my thumb until age seven (I replaced my thumb with a fork), having dark under my eyes (reflecting stomach issues), having impetigo on my face along with other neck, skin, and scalp issues at puberty, not being able to do more than a few sit-ups in high school. As I look back, I see how I was probably only 15 to 20 percent of who I could have been. That applied both to my childhood and my marriage.

But then it all began to naturally correct itself.

My integration of fragments (in Books 1 and 2, it was called the Process of Energetic Change) and my recovery (I call it Return and Restore) included epiphanies, visions, dreams, periods of staring (as if to say "I can't believe this"), journaling, meditation, counseling, trusting myself and my intuition for internal guidance, eating a lot of chocolate, writing, dieting to address my weak, sluggish digestive fire, fixing my poor posture (I didn't know posture affects digestion and breathing!), learning to breathe deeply, learning how to stand up for myself and say how I feel, learning to not be afraid of my feelings, expressing myself easily at all times, no longer being too nice (and setting boundaries accordingly), building a core with exercise and the help of a trainer, experiencing adrenaline issues, feeling my emotions return and my grieving processed, lessening my coping habits (less sugar and fewer sodas, cookies, and crackers).

I was happy my memories were returning, my heavy analytical thinking was subsiding, my fragments were integrating, my allergy to chocolate was ending, my dissociation was fading, my love for color was restoring, my digestive fire was returning, and my stomach issues were resolving.

Hence, I am changing to be the person I always could have been.

A deep understanding of Abuse and Energy is what I needed to know—what all of us need to know—before Peace is possible.

Personal is Universal

When our democracy was founded a long time ago, there was a problem that has never been fully resolved.

In the 18th century, the United States of America was founded on the fundamental idea that *all men are created equal*. But right from the beginning, many did not accept and practice this principle. That's still true in the 21st century. For me, it's another reason why the Anti-Majoritarian Difficulty I learned about in law school caught my attention. The term Anti-Majoritarian Difficulty applied both to ME within my own family and to the conditions within MY COUNTRY.

It was wrong *then* and is still wrong *now*.

Some Americans want to see the old system of Anti-Majoritarian Difficulty—"white man's rule"—stay in place. But as our population has expanded, white men are finding themselves in the minority. Making one of them the face of this minority in a high-profile position was (and is) an attempt to keep the old system in place. True democracy—a system in which everyone is treated equally as the U.S. Constitution states—does not exist for millions of people in the U.S. Still, political factions favor this "white man rule" structure. They do not want inclusion; they want exclusion. They want white nationalism.

In my world, inclusion matters.

In my world, inclusion matters.

A healthy democracy reflects the human body, which naturally has a Left and a Right with both sides being equally strong in character and purpose—with both always seeking to protect the body itself. Balance is achieved this way. Without balance, what happens when you walk down the street and lean too far to the left or too far to the right? You fall over.

Similarly, we need to have balance or we do not go forward. Balance requires each side to be strong and healthy in its own right or stagnation and gridlock result. No one side should ever completely dominate the other. Every day should be an exercise of working together to achieve meaningful forward progress, to rectify issues affecting the common good. Both the physical body and the governmental body *can* become unified, advancing toward a future of equality for all. This is energy— nurturing the energy body as well as the physical body—for the greater good.

Applying principles of democracy to families means no one person should dominate, that everyone is respected and has a voice. Principles articulated in the Bill of Rights can be openly discussed, available, and put into practice every day. That means protests within a family can be justified and protesters respected when they act peacefully. This is also energy.

Our physical bodies tend to be used in one-sided ways, with either the left or right side dominating the other. For example, for right-handed people, the right side of their bodies tend to dominate their left side, their nondominant side. Often, that side is left out or even ignored. And it's most often the emotional side.

For years, the right side of my body was heavily analytical and handled the details of my life. My left side was my emotional, intuitive side and was not actively involved. That has all changed because of the shifts I have made. My active left side is strong while my right side has learned the wisdom of the left side's attributes. My formerly dominant right side didn't have a clue how much trouble my overall body was in. *With my energy shift, it now knows.*

Peace begins on the inside.

And this still applies today. Peace begins on the inside. To solve the divisions in our families, our governments, our country, and our planet, we must first solve the internal division within ourselves. Nurturing our own energy body leads to balance on the inside/outside at every level of our lives—for the outside always reflects the inside.

Abuse of energy is a "divide and conquer" strategy used in war, with emotional abuse being one of the primary tactics. It's an abuse of power that's ruthless, merciless.

So, my Anti-Majoritarian Difficulty fight wasn't only about my authoritarian mother and her enabler, my brother. It's here in our world, and it involves everyone.

24

Restore the Human Energy System

> *If you only see the physical body, you are missing the rest of the equation—the energy body.*

Here is the vision: Empathy returns. True caring for others and the planet surfaces. Authoritarians are deposed. All this because We the People are both strong and determined to govern ourselves based on democratic principles.

Restoring the Human Energy System of innate knowledge and fundamental ways wholly supports us in that endeavor. That's why it's imperative to return to the basics and restore energy systems—for you, for others, and especially for our world.

Return and Restore

It seems like I have been at this my whole life, but it's only since moving back to my hometown before age 40 that substantive changes began. I've learned a lot by calling Survival Mode by its name, seeing my fragments return, and using an internal Flashlight that can be (and is) employed to find my way. We can all build with this Flashlight. It works.

My recovery from emotional abuse began with Return and continues with Restore.

Return is the first and strongest lift for one's self to become truly 100 percent. If you think of yourself like a house with 10 rooms, perhaps you've only been living in one of those rooms for years. Survival Mode has forced you to live in only one. But now, you are about to kick out the "crap" that has filled those empty rooms and live in all the rooms of your expanded house. Nurturing your true self in ways you've not ever done before does this. Speaking out to those who need to hear your words—the ones you've held in possibly for years does this. Say these words diplomatically without going overboard, and you've got this!

You'll recognize signs of Restore when unhealthy ways of coping lessen. For example, you choose to ingest fewer comfort/coping foods and drink less alcohol. You don't binge on movies and TV as much. You cry less often. Your anger recedes. You sense your blockages being cleared and your feelings coming back. Your ability to respond—to speak what you need to say—comes quicker than before. Your physical body adjusts more easily to changes compared to what you experienced during Return. (The Return phase can have bumps such as hives, itching, energy moments that feel like a sting, blue flashes of releasing trauma, allergies ending, emotions returning, weird dreams, even visions, epiphanies, and déjà vu moments.) Your analytical thinking returns to a primary position alongside your intuitive feeling. You *know* you have changed. Your abilities—to feel, to have empathy and compassion, to prevent others from taking advantage of you, and to address your own fiscal, physical, energy, and personal responsibilities—have all increased. They will only get stronger.

Restore means to be in balance. Your nondominant and dominant sides (better known as the left and the right sides) come into balance. To go forward, it takes both sides being equally strong with no weaknesses. Thus, your ability to respond is strong, forthright, yet diplomatic.

You'll know Restore when you get there. It will feel right.

Balance

For years, I didn't feel in balance; I wasn't at home inside myself. To have balance means not living by default. You belong, and you are home because you're operating with the full strength of WHO YOU ARE.

For all those decades, I "made the best of it," whatever my circumstances. But I should have been screaming at the top of my lungs. Now, it is "back to the future" (meaning what I could have been). My advice? Don't hold back . . . don't hold yourself back about anything.

Sometime in January 2020 when my fragments merged after writing the "High School Bus Story" and the "Closing the

Coffin Lid Story," I questioned myself. "Why did I stay behind and not get on that high school bus back in 1965 when I was 16?" Apparently, I wasn't just stuck in the log cabin. A part of me chose to stay. When I asked why (while journaling), three reasons were provided.

1) I had to see this through *whatever it was*.
2) Mom and John needed me even if only minimally *and* even if it would hurt me in the long run by taking up much of my life.
3) It would drive what I had asked for back when I was about 12 or 13—around the time of the initial epiphany when I sensed something was wrong in the house. (See Chapter Fourteen.)

Achieving balance has taken most of my years, but some are left for me to continue, to grow, and to really live. So be it.

Whatever the issues are, they can be fixed by restoring the Human Energy System. That makes it right for individuals, for America, and for our world.

Intuition

The following story shows how intuition can work wonders. Even though I haven't experienced times as financially tough as others, I do know what it's like when the bottom falls out. I had to swim or sink.

Things I Had to Learn the Hard Way— When the Bottom Falls Out Story

I was one of the lucky ones. I never had to live out of my car. I never had to stand in a food line or get food stamps. But at times, I came close to experiencing that. The years 2002 and 2003 were hell.

When I saw a penny on the ground, I knew I had to pick it up. If I wanted clothing, I knew I had to purchase it at the Goodwill I normally donated to. When the church offertory plate came around, I knew I had to fake it. I had zero money to put in. I would cringe. Trusting my intuition became my only option to get out of the financial mess I was in. Who else could I fall back on? After kicking out my presumed safety nets (Mom, my husband, my brother, and my federal government cubicle job), I used most of my savings and tapped into my IRAs to live. I eventually got into credit card debt for the first time in my life. I had to dig myself out of it—on my own. And sink or swim.

Intuitively, I knew I had to pursue a profession with credentials and earn the money I would need for the fight with my brother. I had earned a law degree, found work to pay my school loans, and secured a good-paying federal government job. After I divorced, I dealt with a math error regarding the child support I had to pay my ex-husband, and it drained my savings. My intuition was telling me to take the kids on the kinds of trips we never did when I was married, which further drained my savings. My intuition also told me to quit my cubicle job so I could prepare to write and publish while relying on what savings I had.

Then came "chocolate" and the release of my allergy to it, which led to spending money on what my intuition said I needed. It was right. Because I was shifting, I went through a lot of cash. I even had to hit my IRAs to pay my monthly credit card bill in full.

However, accessing my IRAs brought an income tax penalty from the IRS in 2002. A provision in the IRA tax laws allowed me to convert my traditional IRAs to a Roth IRA over a four-year term, but I couldn't access my IRAs during that time. I did. Boom! Penalty! Ouch! A $15,000 tax bill came due, and I didn't have the funds.

My intuition had me call a local bank where I had an account to ask for a loan. That's when I had an in-depth conversation with a woman banker who said, "Without collateral, no bank loan is possible." (I knew that, but I still had to ask.) Then she offered me a game-changing idea that bought me time until my finances could get worked out. At this time, I was 52 years old with great credit and a law degree. I needed to go with my strengths!

The banker's idea? *To use credit card debt.* She told me to respond to one of the credit card loan offers sent in the mail "but do it right!" First, I was to pay off everything on my existing card before doing a credit card loan with that company. Put NO charges on my current card. Then FREEZE the card—literally. (Some people put the physical card in the freezer, so they can't get at it easily.) Second, I had to find out the terms of the credit card loan (percentage rate, length of time it runs, payment due each month)—and, specifically, how the monthly payment would be calculated, which varies from company to company. Third, she warned me to NEVER EVER miss a payment. Put the monthly payment on automatic withdrawal for the minimum amount and pay more if possible.

Shortly after, a credit card offer came in the mail at a good rate for the life of the loan, a rare occurrence. I read all the fine print over and over. Then I called the company, a well-known Master Card company, and made sure I understood everything. On my next call, I was able to initiate the credit card loan over the phone. I had enough credit to cover the amount of loan I needed, which was enough to cover the IRS tax bill in full.

Even though I had a job at that time, I was making only enough to cover my rent, utilities, car loan, credit card loan, and have a little extra left over. I knew how it felt to not be able to eat. My stomach was in a knot, and I lost 10 pounds, but I had no money for new clothes to fit me. So, one day, I went to my local Goodwill with $75 in my purse and left with a wardrobe that would keep me warm for the coming winter. One item was an extra I couldn't pass up because of its color—a beautiful, long teal blue robe. One problem—it had a stain on it. Still, I tried it on and loved it! But would the stain wash out? Yes!

Over the next four years with the issues about Mom and John, one credit card loan grew to be four credit card loans. Before long, the loans were up to $45,000 including a car loan. It took me four years to pay all of it off. But I did. I've never been in debt since.

Looking back, I see how my analytical brain was on overload, so every decision I made to save myself financially had to be intuition-based. And that worked. It helped me swim—awkwardly at first—and prevented me from sinking.

When have you been proud of following your instincts? Describe what happened.

Here's one more story about the power of intuition.

A Wall of Spices 2001 Story (Revisited in 2020)

Recently revisiting a story I wrote 20+ years ago, I questioned the meaning of the Wall of Spices and particularly its colors. Why the color red? Why the color yellow? Well, both held deep significance at my foundational energy level.

Over two decades, the significance of the red and yellow colors that showed up with those spice labels in 2001 have been further revealed to me. Discovering that my first, second, and third chakras were blocked—and I was a shallow breather because of it—screamed at me. Red, orange, and yellow are the colors for those chakras, respectively. Shallow breathing can exacerbate anxiety because of starving oneself of oxygen needed at those lower levels. That oxygen is needed to function energetically and physically.

In addition, there were the two kitchen potholders my mother had placed with her jewelry from Dad under the log cabin floorboards. As mentioned in Chapter Three, I found them in 2013. One of the potholders was bright yellow; the other bright red.

There was also a photo of Mom and her best friend from childhood with big smiles to greet me in that moment.

There was discovering in early 2020 why I had childhood digestive issues, on again off again as an adult, and how to correct it.

There was a lack of fire in my belly and abdomen where the first, second, and third chakras are located. My body needed spices I'd never used—coriander, cardamon, turmeric, cumin, paprika—to correct and rebuild that missing fire. The spices and their usual foods are red, orange, or yellow. (Today, among my favorites are Chicken Tikka Masala, Leftover Turkey Chili, Tomato Basil Soup, and salsa).

Then there was corrective action by switching from cold drinks to hot or at least room-temperature drinks. A hot tea mix of cumin, coriander, and fennel was included in this arsenal of weapons to correct my lifelong problem. In the original "A Wall of Spices Story," I told about placing my shiny silverware in a cherry-wood chest so the dinner knives showed up all in a line—a show of force. (The original story follows.) Now, I can see the importance of what we eat and how we eat; food can be either part of the problem or part of the solution. And the chest itself was lined in green—the color for the fourth chakra for the heart.

Yellow: the third chakra, the solar plexus. It is also the color for cowardice, for being scared. Chicken. That was me. I was scared of my mother. One time as I was sitting in my place at the kitchen table, my mother held a cast iron frying pan over my head. She threatened to hit me. I heard her words—"I'll brain you"—which left a deep impression on me I'd never forget. *I could not trust her. It was not safe for me in my family home.*

The first four letters of yellow spell the word "yell," but I could not. I was too scared. And who would hear me anyway or stop her when she exerted her control. Hence, Survival Mode crept in.

Red: the first chakra, the root chakra, pelvic floor. It is also the color for empowerment and for anger. Anger serves to block empowerment. Blocking this chakra essentially blocks them all, at least to some degree. This prevents us from getting out of the starting gate and affects us sexually. Again, Survival Mode crept in.

Because details matter, I wondered why it involved the McCormick spices brand. Was it only the yellow and red colors used in their label. Perhaps there was something else? The brand name of the spices was McCormick—the same name of a family that lived in the house Mom rented to us when I returned to our hometown in 1984. The McCormicks lived there when Dad was still alive. Twenty years later, I lived in this house he had built for the next four years. For me, that house was always the McCormick house, a definite tie to my father and the years before he died. Little did I know that during those four years, one of my most significant fragments, the Office Girl, was stuck and waiting at Dad's office in that subdivision just down the street. She was discovered in 2020, my year of clarity. Going deep can yield answers that matter.

A Wall of Spices Story
(Book 1, pages 41-42)

Not long after I started eating chocolate again, I walked into my kitchen and stood in front of the cupboard where I kept my spices. My intuition was telling me to take the spices down from the shelf. I opened the cupboard and removed most of them, but the ones I seemed to want had red and yellow labels—McCormick brand, mostly. The red and yellow colors in the labels seemed to hold a deep significance for me.

As I took each one down, I silently stacked them, one on top of the other, building a wall. *What the heck was I doing?* Yet, I *knew* this was right; I could *feel it* inside. That part of me that had reacted to so many things in the past was clearly at it again. It was proving to be my best friend, as strange as that may sound. But why was I stacking spices this way?

Just before this, I had gone to a Marshall Field's department store (now Macy's) and had bought a cherry-wood silverware chest. Although I'd already purchased the silverware, I hadn't started using it yet, so the pieces were still in the small cardboard boxes they originally came in. I'd never owned a chest for my silverware, and as part of the change initiated by the chocolate, I *felt* it was important for my silverware set to have proper housing.

With the spices now stacked, I got out the recently filled silverware chest and opened it next to the wall of spices I had built. I especially remember noticing how the dinner knives looked in the chest—shiny and new, standing upright in a row looking formidable like weapons—my weapons.

As I looked at the spices and the silverware, I didn't know exactly what was going on. But I *knew for sure* the spices were a wall that, together with the knives, constituted a defense against something—as much of a foe as anything I could ever see. Building this wall was the equivalent of drawing a line in the sand and the knives were a show of force. Doing this felt critically important to me. I was clearly sending a message—but to whom and about what I wasn't sure.

Through this, I was learning about a part of me that can do things on an energy level that goes beyond my ordinary thinking. And even though I couldn't explain this, I could *feel* its significance. This part of me was sending a message—a strong one—in a most fundamental way, making this kind of a wall absolutely necessary.

There could be no mistaking what it meant: *I was going to fight.*

This is how it works. Strange, I know. But learning to understand things by feel (vibration or intuition) is critical. Getting out of Survival Mode and creating a safe environment for any fragments to return was the key for me—and possibly for you.

25

Rise

Energy is at the root of problems, but it's also where we'll find the solutions.

PEACE MUST COME FROM THE INSIDE FIRST, AND ONLY then is there hope for a nation to realize peace.

No more fragmentation. No more divisiveness. No more supremacy of any race. Enough.

A Haunting Memory

As I am writing, Thanksgiving 2020 is approaching, and a haunting memory keeps coming up. Thanksgiving feels different this year. Slowly, I am beginning to realize that, for all those fragments that returned in 2020, this is their first holiday season together in a long time. All that had happened to cause fragmentation decades ago is coming to an end.

Here's my Thanksgiving story that has haunted me since 1965.

Coming Around the Bend— An Obituary Story

Thanksgiving weekend, November 1965. Dad had died in June. I was in my senior year of high school, and only Mom and I lived in the log cabin. John was in his senior year at St. Olaf College in Minnesota. That Thanksgiving, the three of us witnessed a woman—likely in despair after her husband's death—end her life by walking into the path of a moving passenger train. She was the same age as Mom.

John had come home for Thanksgiving by train. The three of us had enjoyed a wonderful Thanksgiving Day dinner at one of the local resorts. I don't have any memory of what else occurred that weekend except for the dinner—and the suicide.

The Sunday after Thanksgiving, Mom and I drove John to the train station in Harvard, Illinois, just over the border from where we lived. I recall standing on the station's crowded platform. Many were talking; we were quiet. We had nothing left to say.

The train would soon come from the left. The tracks had a bend in that direction and tall bushes blocked the view. I could hear the train getting closer to the station. Just as it rounded the bend and began to clear the bushes, I saw a woman with dark hair like Mom's approach the tracks. Without hesitation, she walked from the parking lot to the tracks to exactly where she wanted to go. Then she stepped onto the tracks and turned to face the oncoming diesel engine. She even walked toward it.

The engineer blasted the train's horn and engaged the brakes, but those noises didn't seem to faze her. The back of her long, light-colored winter coat flew up as the train hit her. It was over in seconds. She was gone.

Some screamed. Others gasped. But mostly, people stood in silent disbelief at what they had just seen. So did the three of us. Who was she? How could she do something like that? Why? All sorts of questions went through my head. No answers, of course.

The authorities came and removed her body. It took an hour to get the train—John's train back to Minnesota—on its way again. What had it been like for the new passengers riding in those train cars after what they'd just seen? As for Mom and me, we drove back to the log cabin in silence. No mention of what had happened. Ever.

For a week, I watched the local newspapers for an obituary. Finally, it showed up, giving the woman's name and age. It stated her husband had passed away recently. It was not lost on me that this despondent woman was Mom's age. Mom even owned a long, light-colored winter coat. After suffering emotional abuse from her own mother as a child, after the early death of her father when she was 14, and after losing her husband at age 50, Mom wasn't who *she* could have been.

Years ago, Mom had told me about two events in her life that, when I put them together, shone a light on this. As a child, she delivered newspapers. One foggy night after her last delivery, she was walking home on the train tracks, using them like a road. Because it was foggy, she didn't see a train coming until it crept up on her. She jumped for her life!

The other event happened not long after Dad died. She had considered suicide, even taking the family shotgun to a favorite spot. But she did not act. As she told me, the only reason she didn't was because she had two children to get through college.

None of us ever talked about what we had witnessed that day. Not ever. What we saw, how we felt, how it affected us—none of it. In fact, we never really talked about Dad's death either. We held it all inside.

What events that were traumatic have you never talked about?

For me, this story serves as Mom's obituary. As I wrote it, it helped me say goodbye to her and might have even lifted the dark cloud that hung over her head during her lifetime.

Knowing this—just this alone—has made it hard to stay angry at her.

My Writing Journey

Before I ever began to write, I journaled and meditated. That primed the pump for actual writing to come, especially for my first manuscript I titled *Walls of Silence, Why Our Children Behave the Way They Do*. It was about how food, shelter, and clothing are not enough; more is needed. Looking back, I see there wasn't a stick of emotion in it. Of course, I was describing my own situation without realizing the crucial role energy plays in our lives every day.

Today, I know the oldest of my fragments was the writer. I did not know it then. I realized it in 2020 when the Office Girl was discovered. She had been behind the scenes writing since 1999, conveying words to my conscious mind about what I needed to know. My writing eventually helped *her* to surface and begin to integrate.

When I was writing the first book in this *Abuse & Energy Series*, the rules of energy flow listed in Chapter Twelve came to me. I can see now why they are correct.

Also, in the beginning of this series, I stated how Mom and John weren't "nuts" and that there was another explanation. That, too, is correct. The reason was energy.

But I didn't know any of this when I wrote the *Walls of Silence* manuscript—or even the first book of this series. Over the past 20 years, I learned as I wrote. Today, I can see just how right it all was. How? Because I have experienced the physical and behavioral changes created by going inside and digging myself out of the depths I was in (Survival Mode). That's energy, too.

My Personal Energy Solution

From *Abuse & Energy* to *Peace & Energy*, writing has been my sacred journey, my energy solution. I just had to be willing to pursue it. My hope is that my stories will help you.

Yes, I had an energy problem. But energy was the solution. Bringing home the fragments and trusting myself to do it was my answer.

Energy brought me home.

Abuse harms mercilessly. It causes damage—the kind of damage that can't be repaired without understanding that it even exists. Abuse of any kind renders war on your soul.

But now you know.

And now you also know *you are more than you think you are* and *you know more than you think you do.*

Godspeed. Trust. And live 100 percent.

Mariane's Glossary

Abuse = An abnormal use of energy. For signs of abuse, see article below.
    "Signs of Child Abuse" by William Moore. Medically Reviewed by Hansa D. Bhargava, MD on September 08, 2020. Accessed August 20, 2021: https://www.webmd.com/children/child-abuse-signs#1

All of "This" = The word "This" collectively describes the circumstances you found yourself in and responded to in a way or ways that would help you survive. See Survival Mode.

Built-up energy = Energy that is held within the tissues inside your body; grieving and having unprocessed emotions to release, including all the words you never said and wanted to.

Emotional abuse = A pattern of behaviors that harms a child's emotional well-being and development. This can mean when someone:
- Abuses others, such as a parent, brother, sister, or pet, when the child is around.
- Fails to show love and affection to a child.
- Ignores the child and doesn't give emotional support and guidance.
- Shames, belittles, criticizes, or embarrasses a child.
- Teases, threatens, bullies, or yells at a child.

Dissociation = A person's unconscious attempt at self-protection against an overwhelming and traumatic experience. The mind separates itself from an event or the environment so it can maintain some degree of order and sense. Also, a form of psychological numbing and disengagement; a protective condition; "survival" mode.

Integration = The coming together of not only the body and soul but also all dissociated, split-off parts or pieces of oneself (e.g., dissociated fragments), which return to the body. Allergies ending. Subconscious thoughts merging with conscious thoughts to create an understanding not previously recognized. Also known as the Process of Energetic Change.

Involuntary = In general, as a noun, this refers to the subconscious. It can simply be the many parts of you that *remained present* but stayed quiet for years. It can be *missing energetic pieces* coming back to you. It can be *dissociated pieces* returning. It can also be *information* coming to you from and through other people stemming from their personal agendas.

Isolation = Keeping a child away from others; preventing a child from experiencing social interaction; preventing a child from being around other children or adults to see how others live; a form of emotional abuse.

Negative energy = A low frequency of dark energy. E.g., chaos, division, anger, jealousy.

Pinging = A term used in sonar, meaning to receive a message that has bounced off of an object or anything else; a form of communication with your Deep Self reflecting information about you that you have (in some way) asked to be informed about. An alert to double or triple meanings applied to words, sounds, pictures, or names.

Process of Energetic Change = See Integration.

Recognition = A term relating to noticing, paying attention to, realizing. To me, recognition ultimately meant ignition.

Survival Mode = A deep level of internal suppression; a natural reaction to abuse of any kind; a reaction designed to ensure the individual survives to live another day. It acts like a brake on one's human potential.

Withholding = Not giving someone the emotional, mental, physical, or spiritual support needed to grow in a healthy way; a form of emotional abuse.

Acknowledgments

If anyone had ever asked me if I would write three books (let alone one), I would have said no! And here I am with three! This feat does not happen alone. As *Peace & Energy* completes the series, I am especially grateful to those who helped me over the years to arrive at this point.

Jo Ann Cooper, PhD (met in 1997). She taught me how to trust myself in a way I had not ever done before.

The late **Carol Roberts** (met in 1997). My early spiritual mentor taught me how to journal, how to meditate, and how to find my personal guides.

Members of the Independent Book Publishers Association (IBPA) (formerly Publishers Marketing Association). Beginning in 2000, they taught me the world of book publishing. I continue to work with many of them today.

Attorney Karen Temple (met in 2004) and her staff on Maui. They continually supported me, especially during my long absences dealing with estate issues back in Wisconsin.

Attorney John Bannen (starting in 2005). He took on a seven-year legal fight to resolve my mother's complex estate.

Janice DeCovnick, PhD, Jamie McMillin, and other attendees of the **Maui Writers Retreat and Conference** (2007). Since then, Janice, Jamie, and I have formed a writing group that has encouraged and supported our literary efforts over the years.

Editor Barbara McNichol (met in 2012). She has stayed with me through the birthing of all three books. I am eternally grateful to her and all the others who have brought me to this high point in my career.

After living and working on Maui for more than four years, I feel a part of me is still in Hawaii. Every day of my writing life, the presence of its energy continues to support me.

Peace to you,
Mariane E. Weigley, JD
February 2022

Appendix—Stories in Books 1 & 2

Book 1 Stories:

A Mother's Day Peacock Feather	7
Missing Energy Pieces	27
My Chocolate Allergy	34
My Chocolate Release	36
The Crystal Coffin	37
A Wall of Spices	41
The 9/11 Tragedy	46
USS Greeneville	49
The Iceberg	138
The Second Apartment	140
"What is My Community?"	141
Two Picnic Table Conversations	143
Dad's Funeral in 1965	146
"Mariane, Give Johnny the Toy"	147
Emotional Numbness	150
Discovering WENID	151
A Niacin Release	155
Another Iceberg Rises	157
Suicide Thoughts at Age Fifteen	162

NSF Program Certificate on My Old Bedroom Wall	163
Legs of Cement	166
"Involuntary" Wandering Eyes in the Counselor's Office	169
An "Involuntary" Part Speaks Directly to John	170
The "Ow" Game	174
The Last Straw	175
My "Shoehorn" Relationship	178
Connecting With Me	179
The Pencil	205
Two Places at Once	207
Golden Globe Vision	208

Book 2 Stories:

THE DIVE

I Saw Her	15
The Abuse	18
The Road Back	20
The Old Man with the Lantern	23
Two Power Chairs	26
Family Premonitions	28
My Waxed Kitchen Floor	29
Ugly Boils	31
Exit Wounds	33
Golden Axe	35
Missing Energy Pieces	41
Hundreds of Yellow School Buses	45
The Black Cloud	60
About My Dad	67
My Father's Death and My Delayed Release	69
Almond Butter Jar	71

THE RISE

Power Center Emerges	76
Meaning of "Huh"	80
Going Home Again	84
My First Office Visit	91
Emotional Abuse Pamphlet	93
Crash Helmet Kids	96
Fifty Pairs of Legs	97
One Thing Too Many	103
Connecting with My Past Through Journaling	120
The Martyr in Marriage	138
The Last Straw	139
Off to the Funny Farm	143
The Lurch	145
Bread Knife	147

Recommended Resources

THIS VALUABLE LIST PROVIDES RESOURCES TO ENHANCE your understanding as you explore life's journey. I have included only a sample of books from recommended authors. Please visit their websites for related resources. You are encouraged to add your own recommendations at my website: *www.WeigleyPublications.com.*

Emergency Resources
Healthy Place: Mental Health Support, Resources & Information: *www.Healthyplace.com*
Medical Information: *www.WebMD.com*
National Suicide Prevention Lifeline: *www.Suicidepreventionlifeline.org*
Eye Movement Desensitization and Reprocessing (EMDR) Institute, Inc.: *www.emdr.com*

Energy/Process of Energetic Change
Esther and Jerry Hicks, Authors: *www.abraham-hicks.com*

Ask and It Is Given: Learning to Manifest Your Desires, Hay House, 2004. This book features powerful processes to help you go with the positive flow of life. You'll come to understand how your relationships, health issues, finances, and career concerns are influenced by the Universal laws that govern our time/space reality.

The Law of Attraction: The Basics of the Teachings of Abraham, Hay House, 2006. You'll get acquainted with the Laws that govern this Universe and how to make them work to your advantage. Ultimately, you can learn to take the guesswork out of daily living.

Donna Eden, Author: *www.innersource.net*

Energy Medicine: Balancing Your Body's Energies for Optimal Health, Joy and Vitality (with David Feinstein & Gary Craig), Jeremy P. Tarcher, 2008. This book shows readers how they can understand their body's energy systems to promote healing. It's been called an "enormously practical guide that sings with compassion, integrity, and wisdom."

Energy Medicine for Women: Aligning Your Body's Energies to Boost Your Health and Vitality, TarcherPerigee, 2008. In this companion book to *Energy Medicine*, women can better understand the body's energy systems that will promote healing.

The Promise of Energy Psychology: Revolutionary Tools for Dramatic Personal Change (with David Feinstein & Gary Craig), Jeremy P. Tarcher/The Penguin Group, 2005. You'll learn how to tap into your body's energy, not only to change your health but to change your behaviors and thought patterns.

Robert Bruce, Author: *www.astraldynamics.com*

The Practical Psychic Self-Defense Handbook, Survival Guide: Combat Psychic Attacks, Evil Spirits & Possession, Hampton Roads, 2011. This introduces you to combating the influences of earthbound spirits, deranged ghosts, astral snakes and spiders, demonic spirits, and poltergeists.

It's a highly anecdotal and practical guide to the dark side of the psychic universe.

Lynne McTaggart, Author: *www.lynnemctaggart.com*

Power of Eight: Harnessing the Miraculous Energies of a Small Group to Heal Others, Your Life, and the World, Atria Books, 2018. This is about our miraculous power to heal ourselves, other people, and the world. This power is unleashed when we stop thinking about ourselves and form groups with others.

The Field: The Quest for the Secret Force of the Universe, Harper Perennial, 2008/2012. The author reveals that the human mind and human body are not separate from the environment. Rather, mind and body form a packet of pulsating power interacting with a vast energy sea.

Barbara Ann Brennan, Author: *www.barbarabrennan.com*

Hands of Light: A Guide to Healing Through the Human Energy Field, Bantam, 1988. This hands-on book is a study of the human energy field and how it is intimately connected to a person's health and well-being.

Light Emerging: The Journey of Personal Healing, Bantam, 1993. This book explains the stages of self-care and healing relationships through auric field interaction and higher spiritual realities. Its approach to healing is used with medical therapy.

Nick Ortner, Author: *www.thetappingsolution.com*

The Tapping Solution: A Revolutionary System for Stress-Free Living (*New York Times* bestseller), Hay House, Inc. 2014. 8th ed. Emotional Freedom Techniques (EFT) is an energy-based healing modality that addresses both emotional and physical problems. Using the energy meridians of the body, practitioners tap on specific points while focusing on negative emotions or physical sensations.

Dawson Church, PhD, Author: *www.EFTUniverse.com*

Mind to Matter: The Astonishing Science of How Your Brain Creates Material Reality, Hay House, Inc. 2018. This book shares how to apply the breakthroughs of energy psychology to health and athletic performance through EFT.

Julia Cameron, Author: *www.juliacameronlive.com*

The Artist's Way: A Spiritual Path to Higher Creativity: 25th Anniversary Edition, TarcherPerigee, 2016. This is a proven and invaluable guide to the creative process and living the artist's life. Its message is as vital today as it was 25 years ago, if not more so.

Dealing with Abuse and Codependency

Melody Beattie, Author: *www.melodybeattie.com*

Codependent No More: How to Stop Controlling Others and Start Caring for Yourself, Hazelden, 1986. Recovery has begun for millions because of this straightforward guide. Through examples and exercises, you are shown how attempting to control other people can force them to lose sight of their own needs and happiness.

Beyond Codependency: And Getting Better All the Time, Hazelden, 1989. This follow-up book to Beattie's bestselling classic shows how to continue recovery by developing positive ways of relating to others. Its personal stories and activities provide a framework for individual growth.

Jodie Blanco, Author: *www.jodeeblanco.com*

Please Stop Laughing at Me… One Woman's Inspirational Story, Adams Media, 2010. This unforgettable memoir chronicles how one child was shunned—and sometimes physically abused—by her classmates from elementary school through high school. It is an unflinching look at what it means to be the outcast, how even the most loving parents can get it all wrong, why schools are often unable to prevent disaster, and how bullying has been misunderstood and mishandled by the mental health community.

Please Stop Laughing at Us, Benbella Books, 2011. Jodee Blanco sparked a landmark movement in our nation's schools with her first book. In this compelling sequel, she responds to the demand for more information from teens, parents, educators, and adult survivors like herself who have come to know and trust her as the champion of their cause.

Sam Horn, Author: *www.samhorn.com*

Never Be Bullied Again: Prevent Haters, Trolls and Toxic People from Poisoning Your Life, Cool Gus Publishing, 2015. Full of convincing realism, this book is packed with information and example situations addressing both bullies and their victims. You'll gain ideas on how to deal with both of them.

Personal Growth

Caroline Myss, PhD, Author: *www.myss.com*

Sacred Contracts: Awakening Your Divine Potential, Harmony, 2003. This book explains how to identify your spiritual energies or archetypes—the gatekeepers of your higher purpose—and use them to know what you're here on earth to learn and whom you are meant to meet.

Why People Don't Heal and How They Can (*New York Times* bestseller), Harmony, 1998. This book provides a vital self-healing program for physical and spiritual disorders in Dr. Myss's characteristic no-nonsense style and high-voltage storytelling.

Anatomy of the Spirit: The Seven Stages of Power and Healing (*New York Times* bestseller), Harmony, 1996. Building on wisdom from Hindu, Christian, and Kabbalah traditions, this guide to energy healing reveals the hidden stresses, beliefs, and attitudes that cause illness.

Gabrielle Bernstein, Author: *www.gabbybernstein.com*

The Universe Has Your Back: Transform Fear to Faith, Hay House Inc., 2018. You'll find simple prayers, affirmations, and exercises to support releasing old thought systems and fears. The goal? To stop chasing life and learn to truly live—and return to peace.

Dr. Wayne Dyer, Author: *www.drwaynedyer.com*

Manifest Your Destiny: The Nine Spiritual Principles for Getting Everything You Want, William Morrow Paperbacks, 1998. This classic book teaches you to develop spiritual awareness, reconnect with the world, trust yourself, accept your worth, and let go of demands.

Byron Katie, Author: *https://thework.com/books*

Loving What Is: Four Questions That Can Change Your Life, Three Rivers Press, 1994. Multiple editions. This book is like a cool breeze in a marketplace crowded with advice. The Work will show you step by step, through clear and vivid examples, exactly how to use a revolutionary change process for yourself.

Eckhart Tolle, Author: *www.eckharttolle.com*

The Power of Now: A Guide to Spiritual Enlightenment, New World Library, 2010. This shows how to connect to the indestructible essence of our Being. As Tolle wrote, it's the "eternal, ever present One Life beyond the myriad forms of life that are subject to birth and death."

A New Earth: Awakening to Your Life's Purpose, Penguin, 2008. This book discusses how attachment to the ego creates dysfunction leading to anger, jealousy, and unhappiness. It shows how to awaken to a new state of consciousness and follow the path to a truly fulfilling existence.

Sam Horn, Author: *www.samhorn.com*

Someday Is Not a Day of the Week: Ten Life Hacks for Living Your Best Life Now, St. Martin's Press, 2019. Life is much too precious to postpone. It's time to put yourself in your own story. The good news is, there are "hacks" you can do right now to make your life more of what you want it to be. And you don't have to be selfish, quit your job, or win the lottery to do them. Sam Horn offers actionable, practical advice in short, snappy chapters to show you how to get started on your best life—now.

Meditation/Journaling

Melody Beattie, Author: *www.melodybeattie.com*

Journey to the Heart: Daily Meditations on the Path to Freeing Your Soul, HarperSanFrancisco, 1996. By reading a calendar entry every day, you'll gain comfort and inspiration as you discover your true purpose and connect more deeply with yourself, the creative force, and the magic around and within us.

Tama J. Kieves, Author: *www.tamakieves.com*

A Year Without Fear: 365 Days of Magnificence, TarcherPerigee, 2015. Here are 365 days of inspiration for overcoming fear, conquering obstacles, and achieving your destiny. Also available in audio format.

Marianne Williamson, Author: *https://marianne.com*

A Year of Miracles: Daily Devotions and Reflections, HarperOne, 2015. This offers a daily devotional to help you develop a positive, loving mindset and live your best self in a way that brings miracles into your life.

Dan Harris and Jeffrey Warren with Carlye Adler, Authors: *www.10percenthappier.com*

Meditation for Fidgety Sceptics: A 10% Happier How-to Book, Spiegel & Grau, 2017. The authors embark on a gonzo quest to tackle the misconceptions that keep people from meditating. It's filled with practical meditation instructions—all of which are available on the 10% Happier app.

Rebuilding Your Life When Change Comes

Brené Brown, Author: *https://brenebrown.com*

Rising Strong: How the Ability to Reset Transforms the Way We Live, Love, Parent, and Lead, Random House, 2017. Our stories of struggle can be big or small. Regardless of magnitude or circumstance, the rising strong process is the same: We reckon with our emotions and get curious about what we're feeling; we rumble with our stories until we get to a place of truth; and we live this process, every day, until it becomes a practice and creates nothing short of a revolution in our lives. Rising strong after a fall is how we cultivate wholeheartedness.

Dare to Lead: Brave Work. Tough Conversations. Whole Hearts. Random House, 2018. Brown uses research, stories, and examples to answer tough questions in the no-BS style that millions of readers have come to expect and love. She writes, "One of the most important findings of my career is that daring leadership is a collection of four skill sets that are 100 percent teachable, observable, and measurable. It's learning and unlearning that requires brave work, tough conversations, and showing up with your whole heart. Easy? No. Because choosing courage over comfort is not always our default. Worth it? Always. We want to be brave with our lives and our work. It's why we're here."

Marianne Williamson, Author: *www.marianne.com*

Tears to Triumph: The Spiritual Journey from Suffering to Enlightenment, HarperOne, 2017. In avoiding pain, people avoid their growth. The author offers an opportunity to transform your pain through spiritual healing.

The Gift of Change: Spiritual Guidance for Living Your Best Life, HarperSanFrancisco, 2006. This book delivers hope and healing through 10 basic changes you can make as you learn to view the world through the eyes of love instead of fear.

Dan Millman, Author: *www.peacefulwarrior.com*

Way of the Peaceful Warrior: A Book That Changes Lives, Dan Millman, 1984. This first-person account of the author's odyssey into the realms of light, darkness, mind, body, and spirit has become a bestseller about the universal quest for happiness.

The Laws of Spirit: A Tale of Transformation, HJ Kramer/New World Library, 2001. This book shows how what's at the heart of every religion, culture, and moral system can lead to a deeper sense of meaning, connection, and harmony with the world. It also indicates how these principles can transform relationships, careers, finance, and health.

Louise L. Hay, Author: *www.louisehay.com*

You Can Heal Your Life, Hay House, 1984. This book shares ways to heal, including how Louise cured herself after being diagnosed with cancer. About how negative mental processes can cause physical illness, the author wrote: "If we are willing to do the mental work, almost anything can be healed."

John W. James and Russell Friedman, Authors: *www.griefrecoverymethod.com*

The Grief Recovery Handbook: The Action Program for Moving Beyond Death, Divorce, and Other Losses including Health, Career, and Faith, HarperPerennial, 2009. The authors use their own experiences to illustrate difficulties in recovering. They also provide exercises for writing, calling them "the keys to healing one's grief."

Dr. Bruce Fisher and Dr. Robert Alberti, Authors: *www.drbrucefisher.com*

Rebuilding: When Your Relationship Ends, 3rd edition, Impact Publishers, 2005. A widely used approach to divorce recovery, this "rebuilding" model makes the process healthier and less traumatic for those who are divorcing or divorced—and their children.

Deepak Chopra, MD, Author: *www.deepakchopra.com*

Quantum Healing: Exploring the Frontiers of Mind/Body Medicine, revised, Bantam, 2015. This book offers a fascinating intellectual journey and an updated chronicle of hope and healing based on awareness, consciousness, and meditation. It adds the latest scientific research and Dr. Chopra's thoughts on the body/mind connection.

Martha Beck, Author: *www.marthabeck.com*

Finding Your Own North Star: Claiming the Life You Were Meant to Live, Harmony, 2008. Although every life is unique, major transformations have common elements. This book provides a map to guide you through every stage of change.

Steering by Starlight: The Science and Magic of Finding Your Destiny, Rodale Books, 2009. Using her trademark wisdom, empathy, and engaging style, Martha Beck connects you with proven, effective strategies that have worked for the hundreds of people she has coached.

Tama J. Kieves, Author: *www.tamakieves.com*

Thriving Through Uncertainty: Moving Beyond Fear of the Unknown and Making Change Work for You, TarcherPerigee, 2018. This poetically written book guides you through life's uncertain times. The exercises make you think, feel uncomfortable, and get real. That's exactly what you need to truly make changes and thrive.

Recommended Websites

Institute of Noetic Sciences: *www.noetic.org*
Inspired by a profound experience of personal discovery, Apollo 14 astronaut Dr. Edgar Mitchell created IONS in 1973 to explore the interplay between scientific knowledge and inner knowing.

TED Talk: Brené Brown on Shame
www.ted.com/talks/brene_brown_listening_to_shame

TED Talk: Brené Brown on Vulnerability
www.ted.com/talks/brene_brown_the_power_of_vulnerability

TED Talks in general—search for a topic of interest at *www.Ted.com*

About the Author

Diane Yokes Photography

AS AN INTUITIVE WHO SENSES ENERGY IN A VARIETY of ways, Mariane E. Weigley, JD, writes, speaks, teaches, and publishes what it means to be an energy being. She writes from the soul's perspective that everything is about Energy.

Mariane earned her BBA in business and education from the University of Wisconsin-Madison in 1973 and her JD from Marquette University Law School in 1992. She was a practicing lawyer for 14 years. After her 25-year marriage ended, she turned to counseling, meditation, and journaling. This resulted in a profound shift at the age of 52. As part of her healing process, she began to write—to heal herself and ultimately to lay the groundwork for helping others. *Peace & Energy* is the third book in her *Abuse & Energy*™ *Series*.

Having grown up in Lake Geneva, Wisconsin, Mariane has lived in Hawaii and California. She currently resides in southeastern Wisconsin.

www.ingramcontent.com/pod-product-compliance
Lightning Source LLC
Chambersburg PA
CBHW051940290426
44110CB00015B/2049